The STRESS MANAGEMENT Workbook

A Guide to Developing Resilience

Lynne van Brakel

Teach Yourself ®

The STRESS MANAGEMENT Workbook

Lynne van Brakel

First published in Great Britain in 2014 by Hodder and Stoughton. An Hachette UK company.

First published in US in 2014 by The McGraw-Hill Companies, Inc.

This edition published 2014

Copyright © Lynne van Brakel 2014

The right of Lynne van Brakel to be identified as the Author of the Work has been asserted by her in accordance with the Copyright, Designs and Patents Act 1988.

Database right Hodder & Stoughton (makers)

The *Teach Yourself* name is a registered trademark of Hachette UK.

British Library Cataloguing in Publication Data: a catalogue record for this title is available from the British Library.

Library of Congress Catalog Card Number: on file.

ISBN 9781471801792

10 9 8 7 6 5 4 3 2 1

The publisher has used its best endeavours to ensure that any website addresses referred to in this book are correct and active at the time of going to press. However, the publisher and the author have no responsibility for the websites and can make no guarantee that a site will remain live or that the content will remain relevant, decent or appropriate.

The publisher has made every effort to mark as such all words which it believes to be trademarks. The publisher should also like to make it clear that the presence of a word in the book, whether marked or unmarked, in no way affects its legal status as a trademark.

Every reasonable effort has been made by the publisher to trace the copyright holders of material in this book. Any errors or omissions should be notified in writing to the publisher, who will endeavour to rectify the situation for any reprints and future editions.

Cover image © Cover photograph © Shutterstock.com

Typeset by Cenveo® Publisher Services.

Printed and bound in Great Britain by CPI Group (UK) Ltd., Croydon, CR0 4YY.

John Murray Learning policy is to use papers that are natural, renewable and recyclable products and made from wood grown in sustainable forests. The logging and manufacturing processes are expected to conform to the environmental regulations of the country of origin.

John Murray Learning

338 Euston Road

London NW1 3BH

www.hodder.co.uk

Acknowledgements

Thank you to my husband Rob, my rock. To my loving daughter Louisa along with her partner Danny and my granddaughter Lily, new to the world only 22 months ago.

To my late father John, and my mother Nell who inspired me to work hard for a good life, and my cherished close extended family and friends for their acceptance, support and love over the years.

Thank you to my wonderful colleagues who are also my treasured friends and mentors and particularly to Dena for encouraging me to write this book.

Thank you to Callum McNulty who has created all the illustrations in this workbook.

And finally to all my clients past, present and future for your trust and openness, which leaves me feeling both privileged and humbled. All your revelations are safe with me and your learnings have greatly contributed to my knowledge and life lessons which I will continue to pass on to others.

Contents

Contents

About the author

My name is Lynne. I live by the sea in England with my family. I have a job as an Executive Coach, allowing me to travel the world, meet amazing people and enjoy a rich work/life balance.

I feel very lucky having so far survived the ups and downs of life including two divorces, job loss, family crises, relationship failures, life traumas and loss of loved ones. With hindsight in my pocket I chose to deliberately craft a life which allows me sanctuary, stimulation for learning, and the opportunity to support others in their learning, creativity and challenges.

Professionally speaking, I have been a Leadership and Personal Development Coach since 1990. I have a long history of coaching on leadership programmes at London Business School and I am the Director of a coaching business called Peoplelink. (Lynne@peoplelink.biz)

Before becoming a full-time Executive Coach, I worked in learning and development, management and HR functions while employed with three different government departments and in the private sector. I was also a director of a retail horticultural business and a company employing theatre and performance skills in business.

I have studied in the areas of leadership, coaching, stress and psychotherapy over many years and I am a qualified clinical hypnotherapist. I have post-graduate diplomas in coaching, clinical hypnotherapy, NLP and Counselling.

In my spare time I like spending time with my family and friends, and my hobbies include sailing, riding, writing, gardening and property projects. I am also interested in animals, nature and all things creative, including music and art. I also enjoy coaching young people on business projects.

Everyone has a story; mine is one of striving for balance and integration, nurturing the good bits in life and self-managing the rest. I have developed many practical tools and approaches which I hope will inspire you!

How to use this workbook

In this chapter we will cover:
▶ How this workbook can help you
▶ The structure of the workbook
▶ Different learning styles
▶ Self-managing your learning

Welcome to this workbook!

→ How will this workbook help me?

Whether you are feeling stressed now or just curious about how you can maintain a healthy balance in your life, this book can be of benefit to you. Whatever your stage in life, from young adult through to retirement age, this workbook is designed to help you develop skills to manage stress and develop resilience in order to lead a happier and more fulfilling life.

As human beings we were originally designed to survive, **not** for happiness, but we search endlessly for increased happiness. I have heard many stories over the years which will remain safe with me, but provide invaluable life learnings that are a source of inspiration. I hope these resonate with you as I pass some of them on, together with ideas about how to think, feel and do in response to life's challenges.

If you feel very low or are undergoing psychotherapy or any other kind of therapy this book may not give you all that you need. Indeed it may be important for you to seek or continue with professional help or medical support from your doctor.

However, whatever your circumstances I hope this workbook will help you to:

▶ Identify symptoms of stress;
▶ Analyse situational stress;
▶ Increase self-awareness about how you handle stress;
▶ Provide some strategies and tools for self-managing stress;
▶ Develop your resilience;
▶ Focus on some goals to reinforce your happiness.

→ How to use this workbook

As you are probably already aware, this is not a scientific, academic or technical book about stress, but an opportunity for you to explore your inner and outer worlds to find some real practical strategies for managing your life. If you are doing this already congratulations! This book will add to your sense of success and reinforce the good habits you are already practising and may even give you a new perspective or make sense of your priorities, meaning and purpose.

HEARTS AND MINDS

The ideas and models are grounded in robust research, experience and practical application from which good practice can be applied in business and life. I will also encourage you to use your intuition; a kind of knowing that you have developed over time which is innate in all of us. This is more developed in some than in others, but it emerges when we listen carefully to our minds and our hearts and trust that we know what's best for us. We can also practise this with compassion for ourselves and for others; the journey can feel very different if we have compassion in our lives.

THE STRUCTURE OF THE WORKBOOK

You can use this workbook in different ways.

▶ **Referencing different topics**: Each chapter covers different topics which you can refer to when you have a particular question or need related to that topic.

▶ **Read the whole workbook**: Otherwise, I recommend that you read the whole book to understand how one topic may influence another.

Viewing each situation through a wide informed lens by reading the whole book may help you achieve this.

SELF-REFLECTION EXERCISES

Each chapter contains self-reflection exercises. They are designed to help you learn from your own perspective.

Making sense of how you can relate this to your world will create your own **personalized learning journey**. This is important as it is likely to embed your learning and help you prepare for future action.

CAPTURING YOUR LEARNING

At the end of each chapter you will be given the opportunity to:

▶ **Summarize your learning** – to record the learning that most resonates with you.

▶ **Capture positive thoughts** – based on the idea of Cognitive Behavioural Coaching our thoughts influence what we do, how we respond physically and the way we feel. Capturing and affirming your thoughts is a great way to reinforce learning once you have completed this workbook. Here you can record gentle affirmative messages to yourself which you can continue to carry around with you to use when needed.

If you wish to practise using a thought log, please refer to Chapter 11.

→ Your learning style

Have you ever thought about how you learn?

David A. Kolb, a famous American educational theorist, came up with a model of learning which suggests that we have different learning preferences, broadly fitting into one of the following constructs:

▶ **Activist**
▶ **Reflector**
▶ **Theorist**
▶ **Pragmatist**

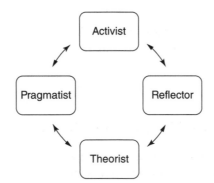

If we take the example of learning to use a new iPad:

▶ The **Activist** will – poke and hope, play around until it works – enjoy the immediate challenge, trial and error and will be very hands on.

▶ **Reflectors** – prefer to watch someone else and learn from observation and have time to reflect and digest.

- ▶ **Theorists** – like to read the manual first. They like the rational approach.
- ▶ **Pragmatists** – are thinking why/what do I need to learn about this and how is it going to help me in the real world? They seek and try out new ideas and are very practical.

 **Exercise 1:**

My learning style

- ▶ How do you usually learn about something new?

_____

- ▶ Which is your preference?

_____

- ▶ Describe an example of your preferred style

_____

 There is no right or wrong – we just have preferences and often learn best using that preference – but Kolb suggests that in order to embed our learning we should aim to take ourselves through the whole cycle. As frustrating as it may be for the *Activist* to sit down and read the manual and as uncomfortable as it may feel for the *Reflector* to take action, it will benefit you to force yourself into the less comfortable zones and help you to have a more rounded experience of your learning. What and how we learn can greatly influence our life choices. Nurturing your own learning is one of the greatest gifts you can give to yourself.

→ Self-managing your learning – a recipe for success!

Self-managing your learning is a skill in itself. Hopefully this book will help you to develop some new habits, or reinforce some old, to help bring about positive changes in your life.

It is very exciting if you embrace this idea; anything is possible if you have the tools to do it!

The **Learning Tools** I will explain are:

1 Self-reflection – your inner and external worlds.

2 Locus of control and self-responsibility.

3 Self-compassion.

4 Flexible thinking and open-mindedness.

5 Trusting your comfort levels.

6 Developing a positive mind-set.

7 Setting realistic and achievable goals.

8 Reviewing learning and celebrating your success!

SELF-REFLECTION – YOUR INNER AND EXTERNAL WORLDS

Your **external world** represents you and how you relate to others, your environment, your culture, social and professional worlds, and the world you inhabit from your perspective. Others' perspectives will be different to yours, but how you relate to your world will impact you and others.

Record in the diagram that follows the influences which impact your external world.

For example:

- Where do you live?

- What is your culture like?

- What is your community and social life like?

- What other things influence your external world?

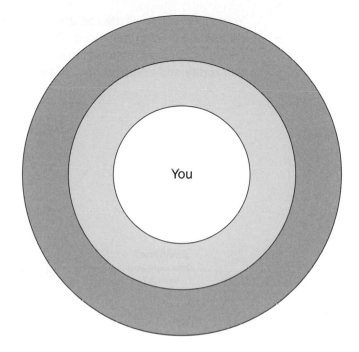

You

What do you notice about this picture of your external world?

_____

_____

_____

_____

_____

 *Exercise 3:*

My internal world

The TAPES Model – Something that happened today...

Your **internal** world is you as a whole person. How you think, feel and physically respond – your responses and your perspectives on life.

Your inner world will also be unique and sometimes changeable depending on circumstances. To warm up before using this model, take a moment of reflection to analyse something that happened to you **today** and complete the four elements of the model for yourself:

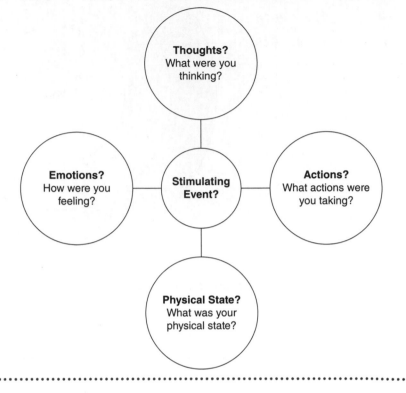

The mnemonic TAPES represents the inner voices and messages which are happening inside of us at any one time.

The external world and TAPES models will be important as a basis for self-reflection throughout the book as a means of measuring how you learn, how you are influenced by others, and how you impact others and respond to demands and circumstances.

LOCUS OF CONTROL AND SELF-RESPONSIBILITY

Who is responsible for my stress?

It is very easy to blame the situation or other people for our stress.

As you read through and reflect on your choices remember that you do have choice if you take responsibility both for your learning and actions in life. You will naturally select those things you decide are important to you and you will focus your energy on these. Trust your instincts to be able to successfully do so.

Put simply, **locus of control** refers to whether or not you perceive you have control over how you respond to events.

SELF-COMPASSION

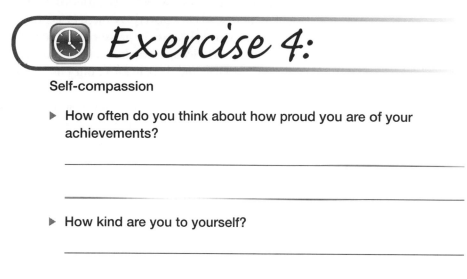

Self-compassion

▶ How often do you think about how proud you are of your achievements?

_____

_____

▶ How kind are you to yourself?

_____

_____

When you are self-reflecting on your experiences, your successes and even your failures I urge you to do so with self-compassion and self-acceptance. You are only human after all and only robots can get it right all the time – and even then technology can fail us!

We grow up in environments which encourage us to be our own worst critics. I'm asking you to do the opposite. Learn and practise being kind to yourself as if you were your own best friend. For example, if we become over anxious about being perfect or imperfect we can worry and agitate ourselves unnecessarily and then, not surprisingly, perform badly. So take what is positive and feels true to you as a support and great development for you and disregard the rest. That's not to say that you don't learn from mistakes but more that you review and understand why they happened and get a plan together to enable you to overcome such situations should they reoccur.

There is more about what compassion means in Chapter 2 and I will integrate these ideas throughout this workbook as we cover the different topics.

FLEXIBLE THINKING AND OPEN-MINDEDNESS

The aim of this book is not to change your personality! We are all unique human beings and if we take our uniqueness away we might become dull, boring and expressionless. We all have differing talents, strengths and passions but often when we overplay these or get too attached to them we get out of balance. It's easy in pressurized situations which we are passionate about to lose our centredness and become extreme in our actions, thoughts and feelings, and this can affect our physical well-being and spoil our experience of life (and also impact others). Being able to step back and discern your sense of centre is another key to successful self-management. If you keep this at the back of your mind as you work through this book you can look for a sense of balance and what might work for you.

 Example: I'm passionate about...

I believe in direct and open communication and if communication isn't transparent it can be one of my stress triggers.

I have learned by experience that not everyone holds the same values about this and discussing differences is more helpful than expressing anger!

 *Exercise 5:*

Passions – a belief you are passionate about?

▶ Write below an example of something you are passionate about.

_____

_____

▶ How would you feel if you were criticized/challenged about this?

_____

_____

This is what I mean by attachment to ideas and beliefs and those most important to us are likely to elicit the strongest defence and sensitivities. Just being aware about what your triggers are will help you manage them.

We can change our habits relatively easily and over time this has an influence in reinforcing the beliefs and values which support us in life rather than those that sabotage us. Knowing what you desire and what is realistically attainable while maintaining balance and enjoying the experiences of life are key ingredients to leading a happy, stimulating and contented life.

Thinking habits can have a huge influence on how you respond. If you practise new habits every day, you have a high chance of changing those habits, so flex those thinking muscles!

TRUSTING YOUR COMFORT LEVELS

As you read through this workbook, manage your own comfort levels as to how deeply you delve and at what level you reflect on the examples you choose to think about. It is possible that some ideas may spark off certain emotions or memories – decide how much you want to open up or protect yourself – it is your choice how you use the techniques and what is most useful to you. Part of the self-management technique is to take responsibility for how and what you think and feel but not to dwell too much on the whys or agonize over how things might have been different in the past. We can't change the past but we can influence how we experience the present and shape the future.

If you ever feel vulnerable place an imaginary cloak or blanket around you to protect yourself from whatever you are feeling or experiencing – it really does work!

DEVELOPING A POSITIVE MIND-SET

We have a chapter on this topic so I won't go into too much detail. The most powerful way we can influence how we perceive a situation and respond to it is to examine how we are thinking about it which then influences and triggers other responses in our bodies. We will work through tools and techniques for doing this.

We will also think about beliefs and habits around negative thinking which can get in the way and block us from moving on.

SETTING REALISTIC AND ACHIEVABLE GOALS

Developing a can-do mentality with realistic optimism is a healthy aspiration! You will have the chance at the end of this book to review your learnings and choose some areas you would like to develop as goals.

Some ground rules in setting goals include:

- ▶ Having a clear vision of where you want to get to.
- ▶ Not trying to achieve too much at once.
- ▶ Working step by step.
- ▶ Having realistic challenges.
- ▶ Developing supports and making sure your environment supports you.

In Chapter 12 we will discuss the specifics of goal setting.

REVIEWING LEARNING AND CELEBRATING YOUR SUCCESS!

This is an important step and one you need to work through methodically to get the most out of this workbook.

Celebrating your success

- ▶ **How many times have you congratulated or rewarded yourself in the last week?**

_____

_____

- ▶ **If you do this regularly well done and keep it up! Why is it so important?**

_____

_____

If we set ourselves small manageable goals every day we can reward ourselves when we achieve them. Practising positive affirmations builds confidence and a sense of resourcefulness which we can learn from and translate into other areas of our lives.

Confidence grows by doing and reviewing.

How we review is critical to self-worth and self-acceptance and another tool to add to your self-compassion tool box!

Summary

- ▶ Read the first few chapters, or skip to a specific chapter if you wish to focus on a specific issue.
- ▶ This workbook contains ideas and exercises to help you embed your learning.
- ▶ At the end of each chapter, you can summarize your learning and capture some positive thoughts.
- ▶ You will have a preferred learning style (activist, reflector, theorist or pragmatist).
- ▶ You can learn to self-manage your internal and external worlds.

My learnings from this chapter

Capture any additional learning points here:

_____

_____

_____

_____

_____

_____

Record these as you go through the book...

Positive thoughts

_____

_____

_____

_____

_____

_____

Where to next?

In the next chapter we will be looking at the big picture and the context of change and how it relates to your world.

1 Stress – the big picture

In this chapter we will cover:
▶ How the world is changing and how this affects us
▶ The inspirational example of Nelson Mandela
▶ A model for managing stress and developing resilience
▶ Our external and internal worlds
▶ Self-management

The world is changing ... do you need to change??

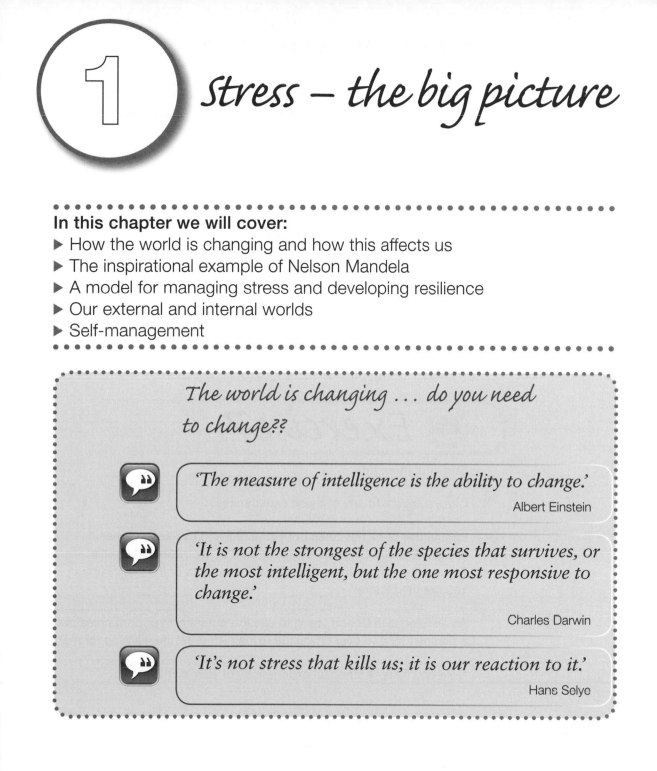

'The measure of intelligence is the ability to change.'

Albert Einstein

'It is not the strongest of the species that survives, or the most intelligent, but the one most responsive to change.'

Charles Darwin

'It's not stress that kills us; it is our reaction to it.'

Hans Selye

→ Stress – the big picture

There are many schools of thought about stress, happiness and developing resilience but what seems to be inescapable is the fact that the world is constantly changing. In the course of our lifetimes evolution appears to be slow, if not irrelevant to us, yet if we open our eyes we can notice change happening around us which has an impact on how we respond to life.

I once shared a humorous conversation with a learned friend about stress who recounted:

'Life can be stressful, getting up and looking in the mirror can be stressful, managing great egos can be stressful, mowing the lawn can be stressful, listening to a boring lecture can be stressful, travelling in a packed train can be stressful, marriage can be stressful! Dating is stressful! Losing your phone can be catastrophic and if it goes off during a meeting … extremely stressful! Trying to lose weight and give up smoking can be stressful; packing for your holiday, unpacking from your holiday can be stressful. Parking can be life threatening…!'

Exercise7:

Stressful moments

Can you relate to any of these experiences?

Writing this book has been both stressful and exciting at times. Imagine Richard Dreyfuss throwing mud at his makeshift Devil's Tower in his lounge in the film *Close Encounters of the Third Kind*. You get the picture!

As an Executive Coach I tend to see the potential in opportunities; as a person I tend to over challenge myself – a great life learning for me!

Note down some stressful experiences of your own…

_____

_____

_____

_____

In life we are faced with demands, challenges and opportunities too. External events are more tangible and easier to identify and relate to; our internal processing and responses are more complex and subjective. How we perceive events and process them internally reflects both how stressed, resilient and happy we may feel.

A very smart client once asked me 'but Lynne, is it really possible to become more resilient?' My reply was and is a definite 'Yes!' As human beings we have an enormous capacity to adapt if we exercise choice.

→ Mandela and his world impact

A very profound example of the human capacity to adapt to his surroundings is Nelson Mandela.

His death in 2013 reminded us how inspirational he was in his ability to come to terms with and adapt to his surroundings during his time in prison.

Whatever your political or religious persuasion it is undeniable that he demonstrated incredible mental and emotional resilience in order to survive the experience. He used his wisdom to influence the fate of millions with his leadership and acceptance of others.

It's impossible to imagine what that might have been like for him. What he certainly did do is manage his environment and conditions around him and self-manage his reactions to those conditions.

Mandela's actions were transformational, I call this the 'ripple effect'; his influence rippling out to others like a drop in an ocean. In the film *Mandela: Long Walk to Freedom* (2013) we can see how he touched people's lives in small ways, for example, the guard in his prison, and in hugely inspirational ways spreading the message for peace, forgiveness and resolution to the wider population.

We can learn a great deal about managing stress and developing resilience from:

▶ His courage and compassion

▶ His ability to self-manage the **external** conditions and **internal** mental/emotional/physical responses

▶ His vision, meaning and purpose

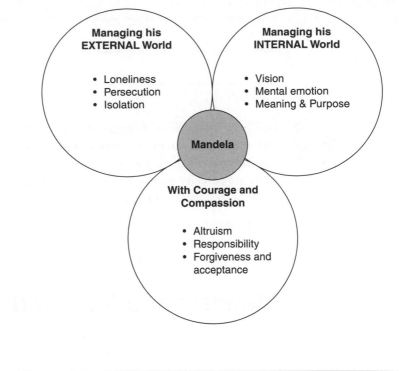

Managing his EXTERNAL World

- Loneliness
- Persecution
- Isolation

Managing his INTERNAL World

- Vision
- Mental emotion
- Meaning & Purpose

Mandela

With Courage and Compassion

- Altruism
- Responsibility
- Forgiveness and acceptance

Exercise 8:

Mandela's story

What else can you learn from Mandela's story?

_____

_____

_____

_____

_____

_____

_____

→ A healthy model for managing stress and developing resilience

Many lessons about managing stress and developing resilience focus on how to manage your responses to events. I will be turning the subject on its head and taking a whole-life approach. To minimize stress and increase resilience and happiness we need to manage both our **external** and **internal** worlds with **courage** and **compassion**. Life can be tough and we can make the journey a very different one if we exercise courage with the choices we make and compassion towards ourselves and others.

Mandela's story was about extreme sacrifice for the sake of others.

Extreme sacrifice may not be what you are looking for in this book. It is OK and wise to act in our own interests sometimes. I call this **'enlightened self-interest'**. I use the analogy of being our own best friend at all times, even when the going gets tough (one could argue it's even more important at these times). When demands come at us, it's easy to try to please others and do more and more to the point where the demands control us.

In the case of relationships we can find ourselves in a situation where we have filled others' emotional tanks and find our own is empty. Not a good recipe for happiness. In order to protect ourselves we need to manage our demands, including demands we make of ourselves so that we don't become saturated and depleted. We are aiming for longevity after all and there is a **'ripple effect'** which occurs naturally when we look after ourselves which then puts us in a greater position of strength to pass on and give to others – a win/win! Enlightened self-interest and courage to make the right choices for you and in the interests of others too, will help you become an enabler for others!

THE RIPPLE EFFECT – A WIN/WIN MODEL!

Courage and Compassion = Acting in the Interests of Yourself and Others - Win/Win!

The model we will be using throughout this workbook reflects the need to manage our **external** and **internal** worlds with **courage** and **compassion**.

→ Our external world – the pace of change

THE GEO-POLITICAL PACE OF CHANGE

In my work as a coach I have noticed with curiosity that reported stress levels have increased particularly over the last ten years. This may have been significantly influenced by environmental factors and world events. In only the last ten years we have had, and are still experiencing:

▶ world financial recession

▶ employment instability

▶ tremendous technological change

▶ terrorist attacks

▶ catastrophic weather disasters

▶ extensive war zones

▶ political, demographic and social change.

For example here are some changes which have taken place over the last 12 years:

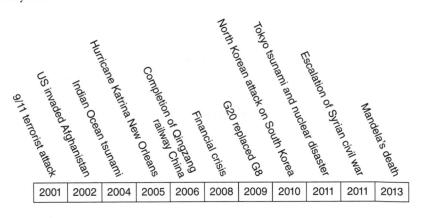

Major global events 2001–2013

THE TECHNOLOGICAL PACE OF CHANGE – 1712 TO 2012

If we go back in history even further over the last 300 years, the amount of change has been phenomenal.

Here are some developments to remind us of the speed of technological change:

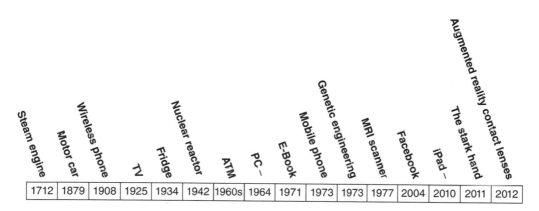

The technological pace of change – 1712 to 2012

Ten years ago, I couldn't have pictured that I would be spending 50 per cent of my time working at home, using Skype, video conferencing, ordering groceries and almost anything else on-line and living in my own 'techno-bubble'!

If you look at the big picture you may also add some other major events which might have occurred in your lifetime and have had a significant impact on you.

Exercise 9:

Changes in the way I live and work?

▶ What changes in the way you live/work have taken place over the last few years?

Timeline

| Last 10 Years | Last 5 Years | Now |

_____

_____

_____

_____

_____

_____

_____

▶ **What impact have these changes had on the way you live/ work/play?**

_____

_____

_____

_____

_____

_____

_____

_____

....

THE PACE OF CHANGE ... YET TO COME?

Experts in various fields are predicting further rapid changes for 2014 and beyond...

▶ Home health monitoring

▶ Renewable energy

▶ Social impact investing

▶ Virtual worlds

▶ 3-D flat panel displays

▶ Speech recognition

▶ Mobile robots

▶ Quantum computing

- ▶ People-powered data
- ▶ Delivery drones

When the **iPad** was introduced there was a kind of mass hysteria to purchase one as it was the 'must-have' latest gadget, and we compare handbag and pocket contents as symbols of our coolness and success.

Advertising and media hype have a big part to play in this, but there are nevertheless social expectations to conform and if we choose, these can be pressures in themselves.

→ What are the social and individual consequences of change?

Social and individual impact of change on the way we live

In addition to the earlier reflections in Exercise 3, have you experienced or noticed any of the following changes in the way you live?

	Yes	No
· Concerns about finances?		
· Virtual relationships – Living with less social contact (and support); virtual relationships replacing real ones?		
· More support for physical tasks – potentially less exercise?		
· Immediate self-gratification – shopping and services		
· Higher expectations for faster, more efficient services and lower tolerance for inadequacies?		
· Changes in work/life balance?		
· Shifts in time, travel and costs?		
· Fewer boundaries between home/work?		

	Yes	No
· *Technology and communications available widely?*		
· *Others?* _____ _____ _____ _____		

→ **The impact of change on the way we work**

 *Exercise 11:*

Changes in the way we work?

Have you experienced or noticed any of the following changes in the way you work?

	Yes	No
· *Less paternalism*		
· *More global*		
· *Virtual teams*		
· *Flexible working – from home, in transit, hot desks*		
· *Increases in population = increases in competition*		
· *Greater mobility and migration*		
· *Others?* _____ _____ _____ _____		

WHAT CAN WE LEARN FROM THIS?

The way the world does business has changed with increasing devolution of responsibility for performance to individuals.

The state or country we live in, organizations and even educational establishments no longer look after us like they used to and career and life management is down to us. Families fight to survive, in some cases on tight budgets and fewer resources.

Young people face difficulties getting the jobs they would like in an increasingly competitive environment and may find themselves under-employed.

Self-imposed demands to be super-busy, super-fit, superheroes can support or sabotage us. The flipside is that there are tremendous opportunities for entrepreneurs, start-ups, change management, leadership, and more interest in portfolio lifestyles with time as the latest currency in making the most of and enjoying the fruits of our efforts.

These factors all have a human impact and create tremendous demands on our ability to adapt and survive and we can feel more anxiety, but also excitement, about the future.

→ **The world we live and work in**

The consequences for the way I live and work

What are the consequences for YOU of changes in the environment now and potentially in the future for the way you live your life? Fill in your answers in the table opposite.

Nature of Change?	Now		Future	
	Positive	Negative	Potential Positive	Potential Negative

→ # Our external world – a danger or an opportunity?

Adapting to change can be a continuous challenge to some or to others an opportunity. Every day newness emerges some of which we cannot anticipate or control and can make us feel uncomfortable when we can't control it. There are the relatively 'safe bets'; such as a planned meeting, a journey perhaps and those surprises or unanticipated events in life which can occur out of the blue; a missed train, a conflict … and maybe a new opportunity!

Our perception of events influences whether we see it negatively or positively.

Exercise 13:

Danger or opportunity?

Consider this list of possible challenges below and tick whether you perceive them to be a positive or a negative:

	Negative?	Positive?
· Driving a car		
· Learning about new technology		
· Presenting to a large group of people		
· Telling someone honestly what you think about their behaviour		
· Changing where you live/work		
· Abseiling		
· Travelling the world		
· Riding a horse		
· Serving the public		
· taking on a responsible job		
· Getting married		
· Taking on a mortgage for a house		
· Climbing a mountain		
· Going to a party		
· Making a mistake		
· Learning a new skill		

If we view demands as a threat we can experience stress.

If we take on too many demands we can become 'saturated'.

If we don't have enough stimulation we can become bored and 'uninspired'.

Balance is a key factor in managing stress and happiness.

→ Our internal world

SO WHAT DO WE NEED AS HUMAN BEINGS TO SURVIVE AND THRIVE?

There are many sources and ideas about recipes for a happy fulfilled life. Among these, the ideas of **Maslow** and **Seligman** are well known.

Maslow

According to humanist psychologist **Abraham Maslow**, we are motivated to act in order to achieve certain needs. Maslow first introduced his concept of a hierarchy of needs in his 1943 paper 'A Theory of Human Motivation' and his subsequent book *Motivation and Personality*. This hierarchy suggests that people are motivated to fulfil basic needs before moving on to other, more advanced needs.

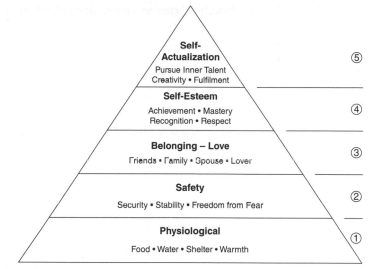

Maslow's hierarchy is most often displayed as a pyramid.

The idea that human needs are hierarchical is difficult to prove and has been challenged by various experts and psychologists over the years, but it is recognized as a popular model of basic human needs for surviving and thriving. It raises some interesting questions about motivation and is designed around a healthy living model of being.

Under excessive stress and pressure we can become imbalanced and destabilized and this hierarchy can collapse while we attend to our lower belonging, safety and physiological needs. When going through relationship break-ups, for example, we may not be thinking about or feeling the need for self-actualization!

 *Exercise 14:*

Maslow and me!

As a general self-reflection exercise, answer the following questions.

▶ **Where do you see yourself on this pyramid?**

_____

_____

_____

► Which stages are most important to you now?

_____

_____

_____

► Are there any stages missing or gaps for you?

_____

_____

_____

► Are you transitioning between any of these stages?

_____

_____

_____

You may remember some good times related to each of these levels and some times which were quite challenging too. The interesting thing about humans is that we seem to look for certainty to feel safe, especially when we go through difficulties, which means that transitioning change can be very confusing and uncomfortable for us.

→ The psychology of happiness and well-being

Although this workbook is about managing stress and developing resilience, it is also about celebrating life and embracing the world we live in, despite the conditions, and perhaps in small, but nevertheless meaningful ways, touching the lives of others and using courage and compassion to do so.

As humans when we face adversity it can bring out the worst and the best in us, but if we manage it well we can emerge with a sense of meaning and purpose intact.

Martin Seligman, a famous psychologist, wrote in his book *Authentic Happiness* that happiness is influenced greatly by the following:

- A pleasant life (pleasures and gratifications)
- An engaged life (in flow using your signature strengths)
- A meaningful life (using your signature strengths and virtues in the service of something much larger than you are)

In his book *Flourish: A Visionary New Understanding of Happiness and Well-being*, Dr Seligman shared a new theory of well-being which he described as the five pillars of well-being, **PERMA**:

- **P** – Positive emotions
- **E** – Engagement
- **R** – Positive relationships
- **M** – Meaning
- **A** – Accomplishment

There is some debate about how physical happiness translates into this model but for the purposes of simplicity I am going to centre happiness, resilience and well-being around how we make choices relating to our whole selves.

→ Counting our blessings

Counting our blessings, having a sense of perspective, meaning and purpose beyond self-interest about what's really important in life, helps us get through difficulty. For some this means supporting your family, having a particular role or vocation in life, being a mentor, or being a good friend, parent or brain surgeon!

We considered Mandela and his world impact, but **meaning** and **purpose** come in many shapes and sizes:

John and Nell

John, in his 80s, lived in an apartment with his beloved wife Nell who was suffering from the slow deterioration of dementia. He had suffered a brain tumour that was successfully removed surgically, but resulted in poor balance. He had very poor eyesight from macular degeneration and was becoming increasingly hard of hearing. Despite his condition, with the help of his family and carers, he made it his meaning and purpose to keep Nell safe. He carried a key to the apartment in his pocket and locked the front door to stop her from wandering, took her to the activities she loved, talked her through each task she had to perform and tolerated her mood swings. He was her brain and she was his eyes and ears. They were hero and heroine together.

Exercise 15:

What do I cherish and value?

If you think about **your** life what do you cherish and value?

Home	Passions

Work	Meaning and purpose

If you don't feel strongly or clear about any of these aspects of your life, perhaps you can come back to reflect on them at the end of this workbook.

→ What can we learn from this?

There is no doubt that the need for self-management is increasing. Additional post-recession pressures to survive financially are squeezing individuals into a zone where increasing demands to deliver more, faster and with greater competition for goods and services prevail. This impacts our lives, our health and the time we have to balance work, play and home. We can be in conflict as we worry about the future and our ability to survive and also desire to profit from opportunities to succeed. For those not working, there can be equally difficult challenges with more emphasis on self-sufficiency and supporting dependants financially and otherwise.

This touch-button world has huge economic and social consequences. We can feel 'squeezed' by the opportunities, as well as by the demands.

THE CALL FOR ACTION AND THE NEED TO SELF-MANAGE

We are all touched by stress at some time or another and have to make life choices every day. However we don't have to endure distress; even in the face of adversity there are always opportunities. We are not necessarily taught these skills and ways of thinking. With the right strategies and mind-set we can soften the impact and protect ourselves from difficult challenges, and harness our courage and take calculated risks when called to action. Life can be tough and the world far from perfect but we can respond with resilience, confidence and a sense of inner peace if we have the personal resources to support ourselves. This workbook will encourage you to embrace self-compassion and compassion for others throughout the journey (a quality which can be buried when experiencing pressure) and to plan your life with forethought and compassionate realism.

In summary, the model of integration below illustrates how we need to take a 360° view on our stress, happiness and developing resilience. It is an ever-changing world and life's learnings are continuous. The more we learn, the greater capacity we have to take on both challenges and opportunities.

The three components comprise all the elements covered in this workbook:

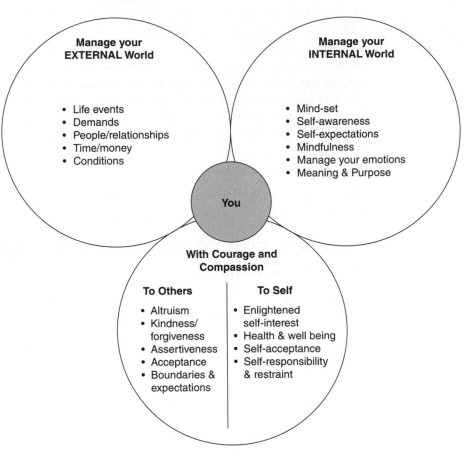

Manage your EXTERNAL World

- Life events
- Demands
- People/relationships
- Time/money
- Conditions

Manage your INTERNAL World

- Mind-set
- Self-awareness
- Self-expectations
- Mindfulness
- Manage your emotions
- Meaning & Purpose

You

With Courage and Compassion

To Others

- Altruism
- Kindness/ forgiveness
- Assertiveness
- Acceptance
- Boundaries & expectations

To Self

- Enlightened self-interest
- Health & well being
- Self-acceptance
- Self-responsibility & restraint

Summary

- ▶ The pace of change is creating many different demands and also opportunities.
- ▶ Our perceptions of how we may view 'challenge' influences how we will manage the stress.
- ▶ If we take on too many demands we become saturated. Too few and we become bored.
- ▶ Counting our blessings, perspective, meaning and purpose help us get over difficulties and encounter happiness.

My learnings from this chapter

_____

_____

_____

_____

_____

_____

Positive thoughts

_____

_____

_____

_____

_____

_____

Where to next?

 In the next chapter we will be looking at how happiness, courage and compassion are defined in terms of stress resolution.

Defining stress, resilience and compassion

In this chapter we will cover:

▶ What is stress?
▶ What happens to us when we are stressed?
▶ What is resilience?
▶ What is compassion?

Picture this ... A near death experience

It was our first sailing trip together; my husband the expert and me the novice on a romantic flotilla trip around the Greek islands. Perfect blue Mediterranean skies and lazy days sailing until one afternoon we sailed around a headland into suddenly and dramatically changed conditions.

The sky went grey and the sea turned black, the large waves menacing, driven by katabatic winds crashing down from each side of the mountains. We were literally caught in a whirlwind. The boat was knocked over flat and hurled from one side to the other. I was helming and filled with panic; I was frozen with fear. I tried to scream but no sound came out ... a silent 'HELP!!' As my husband pulled down the sails my thoughts were – 'I'm going to lose him and then what ... this is it, we are both going to die!' The large dark waves beckoned like a black hole, but he knew what to do and directed me to focus on a taverna situated on the horizon and steer the boat in that direction.... After what seemed an age but was probably seconds I was able to unlock my body, breathe and sail towards the symbol of hope.

→ How does stress affect us?

I had learned about the **Fight /Flight /Freeze** response which can occur when we experience fear. This was the first time I was literally 'frozen with fear ...' To me, it felt like a near death experience. The Fight/Flight responses are automatic responses to perceived danger, designed to save our lives by either standing our ground and fighting, or running away from the situation. I could do neither! The **Freeze** response is an automatic reaction when surveying surroundings for danger in order to make the best decision to maximize survival. I understand this is often experienced by soldiers on the battlefield.

 This example may sound extreme but the irony is that we can perceive many situations in the modern world as life threatening, even though we may not be at physical risk. Over time the excess sugars and chemicals these responses create in the body can cause serious health issues.

It seems that the system designed to save us, is also potentially killing us!

 *Exercise 16*

Can you think of a situation where you found yourself in what felt like a life-threatening situation? What happened? What did you feel?

Event?	Perceived/Real danger zone?	What happened?

EVOLUTION AND OUR CONTEMPORARY WORLDS

In our early evolution we were often at physical risk and literally faced daily life-threatening situations. The bodily response to threat was to gear up for the fight or run like hell and the stress hormones and sugars we automatically produced brought us into a state of red alert; the hard wiring we often refer to as **Fight/Flight**. There was another step when faced with a sabre toothed tiger – **Freeze**. The freeze response allowed us to survey for the nearest safe rock to hide behind, weapon or whatever strategy seemed to be the best to survive. Hopefully if all went well we did survive and had a nice rest afterwards around the camp fire. We would have used up so much physical energy to deal with the situation that we were probably quite tired and in need of recovery time.

AND NOW...

If you stretch your imagination back to 'Primitive Tribal' versus 'Modern Living' we see a very sharp contrast to the hunter gatherer rhythmic, ritualistic simplicity and the modern day multi-taskers, multi-roled, multi-challenged individuals we have become. That's not to say it was easy back in those days and even now many of the world's population struggle to survive. In the modern world our desire to survive and thrive is the same, but in entirely different circumstances to those of our ancestors which is sometimes at odds with our primal instincts.

THE CAR PARK

I vowed never to enter my local car park on the first day of the sales again, having witnessed faces of rage and weapons of mass destruction (cars) fighting for the last parking space.

The difference between the 'Car Park' and the 'Sabre Toothed Tiger' scenario is that we fight or run from the tiger to save our lives and the lack of car parking space is just an inconvenience. In the driving seat or passenger seat of the car, we risk full-blown physical road rage with nowhere for the energy to go!

We may get that parking space and feel good about it immediately afterwards, but may have to deal with the health risks and, if we act out our road rage, the social and legal consequences, not to mention the internal guilt and remorse which is likely to kick in within a few minutes during the calming down phase.

On a more everyday level, being late for a meeting and the social concerns of the imagined consequences could feel life threatening.

The drive to get the latest gadget, or trying to please others at all costs are just simple examples of how we can make demands of ourselves and others and experience **Fight/Flight/Freeze** in non-life-threatening situations.

Of course if we are able to step back and exercise emotional control and detachment, we may be able to avoid feelings of rage altogether, but we haven't covered this yet and we all have our **Hot Buttons!**

→ Our perception of danger

The responses to every day stressors (or **Triggers**) may not be so extreme but unchecked can insidiously creep up on us until we become overwhelmed, over-challenged, depressed and seriously ill.

OUR BRAINS

One explanation for the disconnect between what we see as a threat and reality, is the way that our brains have evolved over millions of years.

We now have 'three' brains:

The primitive brain

This is also called the reptilian brain and is mainly designed for survival. It sends the red alert messages when faced with 'The Sabre Toothed Tiger' or 'Car Parking Space' scenarios! In perceived stressful situations, this part of the brain takes over.

The mammalian brain

This is also referred to as the limbic brain. This evolved later in our evolution and is designed for making connections, nurturing, intimacy, pleasure, spirituality, ability and emotions.

The neocortex

This is the newest part of the brain and is in charge of abstract thinking, analysing and making decisions.

Clearly, relying on our **reptilian** brain isn't always best in terms of making choices and from a health perspective. Understanding our responses to different **triggers** will minimize the harmful effects and increase potential for greater well-being.

Exercise 17:

What does the word 'stress' mean?

What does the word 'stress' mean to you? Record your answers on the diagram below.

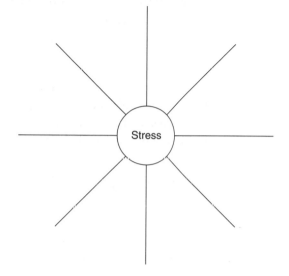

Here are some responses to the same question from other people I surveyed:

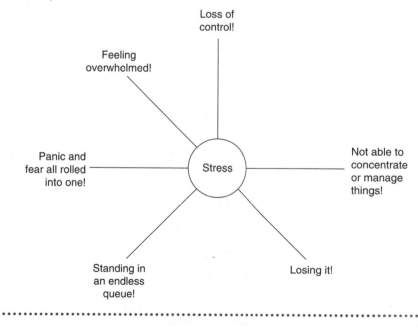

Clearly the experience of stress is subjective but there are also commonalities and the most commonly accepted definition of stress (mainly attributed to **Richard S Lazarus**) is that:

> *Stress is a condition or feeling experienced when a person perceives that demands exceed the personal and social resources the individual is able to mobilize.*

People feel little stress when they have the time, experience and resources to manage a situation. They feel great stress when they think they can't handle the demands put upon them. It is not an inevitable consequence of an event; it depends a lot on people's perceptions of a situation and their real ability to cope with it.

→ Stress response

We all have our own **triggers**.

Triggers are the event, situation, person or perceived danger which if seen as a threat, creates a reactive cycle starting with a thought which turns into a feeling, a physical reaction and an action.

It starts with a…

Stress trigger ⟶ Response

… and stress triggers can relate to either an **external** or **internal** trigger.

EXAMPLES OF EXTERNAL TRIGGERS

External triggers:

Tick those which trigger a stress response in you	✔
• Finances	
• Job security	
• Family relationships	
• Queuing	
• Impoliteness	
• Lateness	
• Conflict with others	

· Add some of your own examples . . .	
·	
·	
·	

EXAMPLES OF INTERNAL TRIGGERS

Other triggers are internal demands we place upon ourselves like:

Internal triggers

Tick those which trigger a stress response in you	✓
· Trying to be perfect	
· Pleasing others	
· Being productive	
· Avoid wasting time at all costs	
· Worries about our children	
· Worries about our parents	
· Worries about our futures	
· Worries about our ability to survive	
· Worries about being good enough	
· Worries about what our friends think of us	
· Add some of your own examples . . .	
·	
·	
·	

→ What happens to us when we are stressed?

Exercise 18:

Response to stress.

What happens to your body when you are stressed? Using the blank figure below, record how you look and feel when you are stressed.

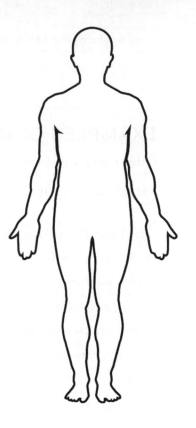

Humanoid

Here is what happens in summary:

Stress trigger   External and/or internal triggers

↓

If perceived as a threat   Message is received through the senses to the amygdala (which contributes to emotional processing). The message is carried along the cerebral cortex to the hypothalamus (the command centre).

↓

Fight/freeze/flight response   Arousal of **A**utomatic **N**ervous **S**ystem
ANS controls heart, lungs, stomach, blood vessels and glands
ANS consists of two different systems:
- Parasympathetic nervous system – chemical messages via neurotransmitters conserves energy levels and increases bodily secretions
- Sympathetic nervous system prepares body for action

↓

Physiological imbalance

↓

Effects on performance and long-term health
- Positive
- Negative

Your humanoid may look similar to this one:

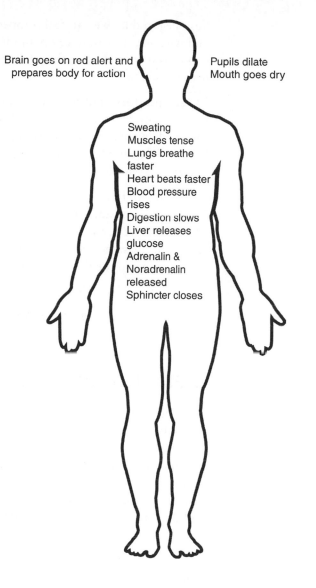

Brain goes on red alert and prepares body for action

Pupils dilate
Mouth goes dry

Sweating
Muscles tense
Lungs breathe faster
Heart beats faster
Blood pressure rises
Digestion slows
Liver releases glucose
Adrenalin & Noradrenalin released
Sphincter closes

Humanoid

→ Mind over matter

Is stress inevitable?

When it comes to saving our lives and responding to physical threats we need the chemicals, fats, sugars and energy to see us through but when it comes to non-life threatening situations stress is not inevitable. Worry is designed to alert us to possible issues which need to be resolved but when the sources are blind spots or are 'non-negotiable' we can feel trapped and cornered. By applying vision and wisdom, we can develop mindful strategies to help prepare and choose our responses, rather than being victims to those automatic learned reactions.

My sailing story continued with me competing in the Laser 2000 national competition three years later in gale force winds. While the winds were at times unmanageable, I nevertheless felt in control because I knew what I was doing and what to expect – it was an amazing experience!

Fears can paralyse or mobilize us. The good news is that once we have been to the edge and survived, the threats don't seem so threatening anymore. If we revisit our original source of fear it doesn't hold us captive in the same way again. In other words we can learn from our experiences and use the knowledge to reframe how we perceive a threat.

Is it really a threat?   Familiarity ⇩ + ⇧ Mindfulness

→ Defining stress and happiness

Defining stress is a real challenge in itself as we all have different ideas and vulnerabilities around stress. Happiness could be said to be the opposite to stress but this is not necessarily so as by reducing stress we don't automatically increase happiness. The two can co-exist. We may be feeling very stressed about a particular issue but overall full of gratitude in other aspects of our lives. We also have good days and bad days, the week from hell, short-term crisis and longer-term stress.

However, our aim is to reduce stress and increase happiness; by self-managing demands we can build resilience and make more space for happiness.

→ 'What is resilience?'

⏱ Exercise 19:

What does resilience mean?

What does the word resilience mean to you? Record your answers on the diagram that follows.

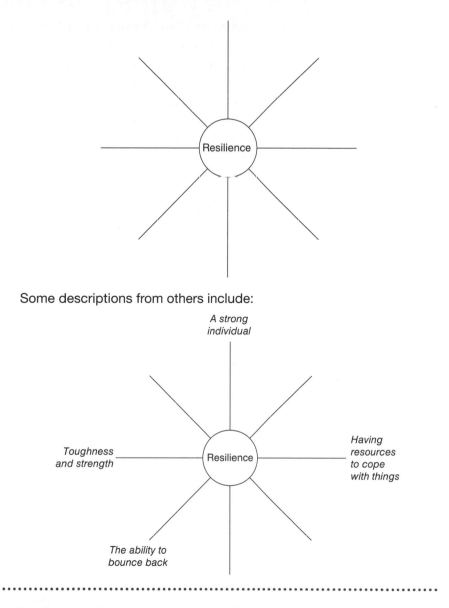

Some descriptions from others include:

A strong individual

Toughness and strength

Resilience

Having resources to cope with things

The ability to bounce back

Resilience is the capacity to withstand stress and catastrophe. Psychologists have long recognized the capabilities of humans to adapt and overcome risk and adversity. Individuals and communities are able to rebuild their lives even after devastating tragedies. Consider the tsunamis of recent years, 9/11 and other acts of terrorism and, at a more personal level, my mother after losing her beloved husband coping so admirably with a nursing home and dementia. We all have stories about people we admire deeply; our heroes and heroines.

Being resilient doesn't mean going through life without experiencing stress and pain. People feel grief, sadness, and a range of other emotions after adversity and loss. The road to resilience lies in working through the emotions and effects of stress and painful events.

Resilience is also not something that you're either born with or not. Resilience develops as people grow up and gain better thinking and self-management skills and more knowledge. Resilience also comes from supportive relationships with parents, peers and others, as well as cultural beliefs and traditions that help people cope with the inevitable bumps in life. Resilience is found in a variety of behaviours, thoughts, and actions that can be learned and developed across the life span.

HERE ARE SOME FACTORS THAT CONTRIBUTE TO RESILIENCE

Tick those that you feel you are good at, or those that you feel you could develop:

	Good at	Could develop
· Close relationships with partner, family and friends		
· Exposure to risks to gain familiarity and learning from experience		
· A positive view of yourself and confidence in your strengths and abilities		
· Managing strong feelings and impulses		
· Good problem-solving and communication skills		
· Feeling in control		
· Seeking help and getting resources		
· Making choices rather than being a victim		
· Coping with stress in healthy ways and avoiding harmful coping strategies		
· Helping others		
· Finding positive meaning in your life despite difficult or traumatic events		

We have many ways of overcoming adversity.

Resilience is the capacity to adapt successfully in the face of threats or disaster. People can improve their capacity for resilience at any time of life.

Exercise 20

Think back to an experience where you felt supremely resilient:

- ▶ **What was happening around you?**
- ▶ **What were you doing?**
- ▶ **How were you feeling?**
- ▶ **What were you hearing?**
- ▶ **What were you thinking?**
- ▶ **What were you seeing?**

How many of these strategies do you employ?

_____

_____

_____

_____

_____

We all have some good experiences of being resilient when we may have felt supremely confident. In other words, we have the resources to be resilient if we choose the right mind-set.

→ What is compassion?

Compassion involves practising the following on yourself and others:

	Good at	Could develop
• Compassion		
• Forgiveness		
• Resistance to impulse		
• Kindness		
• Awareness of acceptance and self-criticism		
• Altruism		

· Fairness		
· Attention to health and well-being		
· Tolerating own emotions		
· Courage		

And there may be other areas of your life where you can practise compassion too!

YOUR EXPERIENCE OF COMPASSION

Describe some of your experiences of others showing compassion to you and the impact it had on you in each of the areas below:

Impact on me	Example
· Forgiveness	
· Resistance to impulse	
· Kindness	
· Awareness of judge-mentalism	
· Altruism	
· Fairness	
· Attention to health and well-being	
· Tolerating own emotions	
· Courage	
· Others	

_____
_____
_____

I hope your examples inform you that showing compassion often takes courage and discipline and is not about being soft and cuddly.

Example: Too many sweets?

Sometimes when we are acting in both our own interests and in the interests of others we have to see past immediate gratification and popularity.

Giving children too many sweets may make you very popular and relieve the demands of the moment, but long term it may not be in the child's interests either from a health or teaching them self-control perspective.

Leadership often involves making unpopular decisions and can cause inner conflict about in whose interests decisions may be. Leading with integrity and looking to long-term interests may override short-term needs.

Compassion acknowledges our humanness, fallibility and vulnerability.

SKILLS OF COMPASSION

Whatever challenges we find ourselves facing or messages delivering we can do so with compassion. Some of the skills involved in communicating with compassion are:

(Tick those skills which you feel you do well and place a '?' on those you could develop more)

	Good at	Could develop
• Reflecting and preparation		
• Setting boundaries and expectations		
• Showing empathy		
• Managing own emotions		
• Managing blame, denial and self-criticism		
• Caring		
• Holding attention and mindfulness		
• Conflict resolution and harmonizing		
• Healing and soothing		
• Offering support		
• Listening and counselling		

	Good at	Could develop
· Coaching and mentoring		
· Informing and communicating		
· Showing respect for others		

I will integrate these ideas throughout this workbook as we cover the different topics.

→ What is self-management?

Here are some ideas about self-management. Again, tick those you are good at and those you could develop.

Self-management		
	Good at	Could develop
· Being self-aware and conscious of your internal triggers and responses to demands		
· Deciding how you wish to respond		
· Deciding where you want to focus your energy		
· Setting yourself realistic and achievable goals		
· Being kind to yourself		
· Recognizing you have choice to be, to have and to do the things you choose to		
· Taking control over those demands rather than letting them control you		
· Taking responsibility for your own well-being		
· Practising 'enlightened self-interest' (nobody will ever take care of you the way you can)		
· Making choices about the giving to others/receiving from others you do		
· Honest clear communication with compassion, from the heart		
· Using your talents and strengths to help you feel more fulfilled and to give willingly to others		
Asserting boundaries and expectations when needed		

Summary

- ▶ The fight/flight/freeze response occurs when we sense or perceive danger.

- ▶ We all have our own internal and external stress triggers.

- ▶ By stepping back and thinking about what we perceive as a threat we can choose alternative responses leading to greater resilience.

- ▶ Compassion supports resilience and helps us to think more realistically about what we can expect from ourselves and others.

- ▶ Self-management involves being self-aware and making choices which are positive for you and for others.

My learnings from this chapter

_____

_____

_____

_____

_____

_____

Positive thoughts

_____

_____

_____

_____

_____

_____

Where to next?

In the next chapter we will look at how you can self-diagnose your stress and happiness, verify their sources and develop self-management goals.

Diagnosis and stock check

Carl's story

Carl was a successful Vice President of a consulting organization. He had enjoyed a golden career; the Beckham of the consulting world. As a Harvard graduate, he had rapidly made his way up the corporate ladder. He had a lovely wife and two gorgeous young daughters. He thought he should be happy but felt miserable. The last two years had been the most challenging of his life. He had been working long hours and was worried about maintaining his position in the company, particularly as post-recession business was tough and he had a huge mortgage. He also experienced a great loss when his father died and worried about how his mother was coping. He had little time with his family and felt sick, trapped and exhausted. His confidence in his ability to cope was sliding away as he rarely felt 'good enough' and couldn't see a way out … and now the last straw; his house sale had just collapsed!

Just one thing after another!

→ The cumulative effect ...

This isn't such an unusual story about how working hard and over-challenging ourselves can get out of balance and what seemed like good opportunities in the first place became a huge burden and weight to carry. It's also a story about how one event after another can build up until the last straw leaves us feeling completely overwhelmed and unable to cope. You could say 'lucky him – at least he has money' but happiness is relative and not necessarily attached to wealth.

I have noticed that at least 90 per cent of my coachees report that they are either currently experiencing some degree of stress or have done so at different points in their lives. This gives me empirical evidence that stress ebbs and flows as we navigate through the highs and lows of life. This is normal and a sense of healthy realism is more likely to help us accept that we are human after all and that the world is imperfect. We can't always anticipate what's coming to us, good or bad. But we can be more self-aware and gentle on ourselves and get the support when we need it.

This chapter will help you take a **stock check** on how you are feeling at the moment and help you develop some self-management goals to help you rebalance or maintain balance

→ Remember to practise acceptance!

So I imagine you thinking ...

▶ 'Where am I on the stress barometer?'

▶ 'Am I normal?'

▶ 'Do I have issues /problems I wasn't aware of?'

▶ 'Should I worry about this more?'

As human beings we focus naturally on disturbances and then get **disturbed** by our disturbances! So as you work through this chapter practise **acceptance**!

Acceptance of yourself as a unique human being without the need to compare yourself to others, to label or castigate yourself but from a position of curiosity and interest in understanding yourself more.

We will look at your world and what challenges you face and do a self-diagnosis to identify the source of those challenges and the level of balance you have in your life.

We will also consider what brings you joy and pleasure and meaning in your life – remember stress and happiness can co-exist!

→ Diagnosis 1 – work/life balance

This pie chart is an example of how we might divide our time between the things we value.

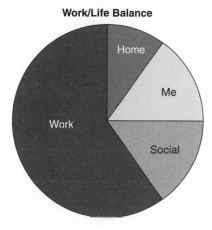

Work/Life Balance

LET'S CONSIDER:

▸ Your work/life balance

▸ Your stress and happiness levels

Exercise 21:

Work/life balance

▸ Can you draw a pie chart of how you spend your time now?

Work/Life Balance

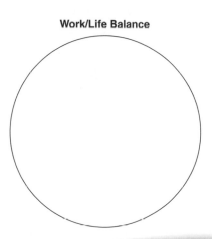

▶ Where does your energy go – how does this influence your time?

_____

_____

_____

_____

_____

▶ What do you value in life – how does this chart reflect these values?

_____

_____

_____

_____

_____

▶ What would you like the work/life pie chart to look like?

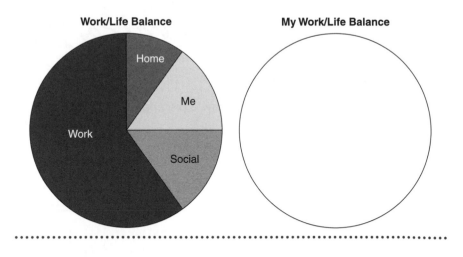

→ Diagnosis 2 – stress and happiness levels

Feelings are our feedback and give us an important gauge for measuring our stress and happiness levels. Others may also bear witness to our behaviours and physicality, particularly our friends and loved ones! We typically rise and fall in stress and happiness levels depending on what's going on in our lives and how we are self-managing.

Exercise 22:

My stress and happiness scale scores.

Let's start with a Stress/Happiness barometer. Indicate on the scales below how Stressed/Happy you feel in your life now.

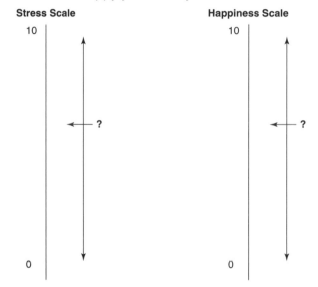

Now that you have scored yourself make a few bullet points beside each scale about why you scored yourself at that level. This may include present issues in your life, work demands, challenges or even opportunities which are presenting themselves to you.

⏱ *Exercise 23:*

How did you score on stress?

Consider the following questions on **Stress Scale**.

▶ What influenced your stress score?

_____

_____

_____

▶ Why is your stress score at this level now?

_____

_____

_____

▶ How long has it been at this level?

_____

_____

_____

▶ If there have been fluctuations what has influenced those fluctuations?

_____

_____

_____

▶ If you wanted to reduce this score what would it take to do so?

_____

_____

_____

Exercise 24:

How did you score on happiness?

▶ What influenced your happiness score?

_____

_____

_____

_____

▶ Why is your happiness score at this level now?

_____

_____

_____

_____

▶ How long has it been at this level?

_____

_____

_____

_____

▶ If there have been fluctuations what has influenced those fluctuations?

_____

_____

_____

_____

▶ If you wanted to increase this score what would it take to do so?

_____

_____

_____

_____

··

STRESS SCORES

If you have **high scores** on the **stress** side then this gives you some feedback to pay some extra attention to what is happening to you in your life and why.

If your **stress** scores are **low** you may ask yourself how you can maintain this.

HAPPINESS SCORES

If your **scores** are **high** that's brilliant! We still need to pay attention though to why those scores are high and how to maintain happiness and the conditions we need to support it. Yes, this self-management business takes continuous work and self-awareness!

If they are **lower,** then asking yourself specifically why that is will help you create some movement towards taking some action to remedy the situations you face.

But … be alert!

Conditions can change quickly so being prepared and mindful about how you respond to the external environment will help you succeed in maintaining a balanced scorecard!

→ Diagnosis 3 – sources of stress and happiness

Exercise 25:

Which areas are important to you?

Complete your own **Mind Map** below to identify those areas which are important to you.

What are the issues which are bothering you or you may wish to develop?

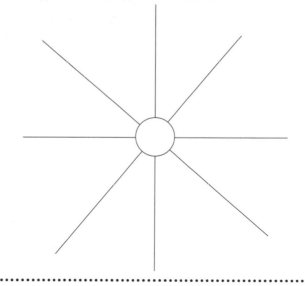

SELF-SCORING

Some of the above you will feel strongly about and others less so. To help you identify the strength of importance of these, give yourself some scores (0–10) for each area.

SOME BROAD SOURCES OF STRESS AND HAPPINESS

If you find it difficult thinking about why you gave yourself the scores you did, here are a few ideas about some typical life influences.

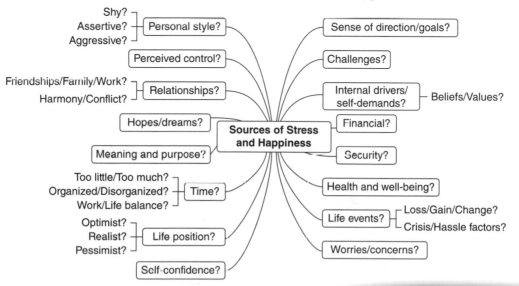

→ Diagnosis 4 – symptoms of stress and happiness

Symptoms of stress/happiness

Do you recognize any of these symptoms?

THOUGHTS

Stress symptoms	✓/x	Happiness symptoms	✓/x
· Rigid and extreme thinking		· Flexible thinking	
· 'I can't stand it if my performance/ conditions don't match my demands'		· I accept my fallibility and am prepared to adapt to the circumstances	
· I must/should/have to....(e.g.) Be liked... Be perfect... Be in control...		· I choose my relationships	
· Low frustration tolerance		· I am the judge of my own worth	
· Catastrophizing		· I'm human and can try my best	
· Paranoia		· I recognize what I can/can't control	
· Confused		· I keep a perspective and can let unimportant issues go	
· Others		· I take a realistic/balanced approach to life	
		· I have a clear focus	
		· Others	

ACTIONS

Stress symptoms	✓/x	Happiness symptoms	✓/x
· Direct aggression		· Assertive	
· Indirect aggression		· Compassionate	
· Overly competitive		· Courageous	

	✓/✗		✓/✗
· Helplessness		· Collaborative	
· Hurrying/rushing/talking fast		· Self-responsibility	
· Compulsive		· Pace myself	
· Avoidance		· Organized	
· Disorganized		· Constructive	
· Irritable		· Confident	
· Distracted/poor attention and focus		· Others	
· Closed body language			
· Withdrawn			
· Others			

PHYSICAL

Stress Symptoms	✓/✗	Happiness Symptoms	✓/✗
· Tired		· High energy	
· Low energy		· Focused energy	
· Sleep disturbance		· Centred	
· Restlessness		· Relaxed and in-flow	
· Tension/tight muscles		· Physically fit	
· Muscle spasms/tics		· Balanced diet	
· Loss of appetite/overeating		· Healthy weight, stamina, exercise, flexible	
· Aches and pains		· Regular relaxation	
· Headaches		· Healthy blood pressure	
· Teeth grinding		· Stimulated/alert	
· Panic attacks		· Sleep well	
· Sweating		· Open body language	

	✓/x	• Others	
• Abdominal pains			
• Nausea			
• Allergies			
• Skin conditions			
• Diarrhoea/constipation			
• Biological illness (cancer, diabetes, arthritis, high blood pressure, asthma)			
• Lowered immune system			
• Burnout			
• Others			

EMOTIONS

Stress symptoms	✓/x	Happiness symptoms	✓/x
• Anger		• Joy	
• Frustration		• Hopeful	
• Crying		• Confident	
• Sadness		• Happy	
• Jealousy		• Resourceful	
• Shame		• Pride	
• Lack of confidence		• Excited	
• Paranoia		• Stimulated	
• Hurt		• Others	
• Guilt			
• Depression			
• Suicidal feelings			
• Others			

DEPRESSION – SYMPTOMS

We all have negative feelings and mood dips but if the following symptoms persist and override your positive experience of life over a longer period of time you may be experiencing depression:

▶ Having little pleasure or interest in doing things

▶ Feeling down, depressed or hopeless

▶ Having trouble sleeping or sleeping too much

▶ Feeling tired/little energy

▶ Poor appetite or over-eating

▶ Feeling like a failure

▶ Problems concentrating

▶ Movements slow or fidgety

▶ Having suicidal or self-harm thoughts

Health Warning!

If you are feeling depressed, your job is to take yourself to the doctor.

Nothing will change until you take these first steps to ensure you get a proper diagnosis.

Without your health you cannot function, so this is the first step to building your resilience.

→ Diagnosis 5 – stress, happiness and your performance

Change offers challenge and opportunity. Sometimes in the pursuit of opportunities we can take too much on. If we take on too many challenges we can become saturated and performance goes down. If we don't have enough we risk being bored and disaffected. **Balance** is the key to self-management; we need to work out which challenges are good for us and which could be negative, and find the zones where we can feel stimulated and motivated.

WHERE ARE YOU ON THIS PERFORMANCE CURVE?

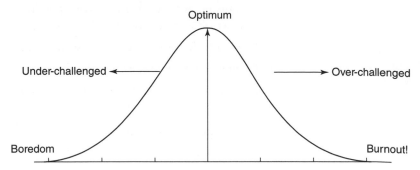

Optimum

Under-challenged ←

→ Over-challenged

Boredom

Burnout!

Our perception of what we must have and what we must do can result in the external demands controlling us rather than us controlling them.

DEMANDS – CARL'S STORY

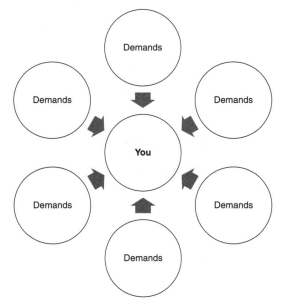

Negative saturation – 'Them controlling us'

When we take on too many demands, we can become saturated and over time in an effort to keep up and keep giving, we burn ourselves out! Carl is a good example of this.

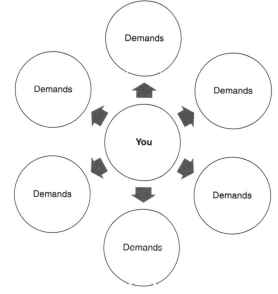

Positive – 'Us controlling them'

Carl's recovery from burnout involved him taking control of the demands, protecting himself from the excesses and rebalancing his perception of what he could and couldn't do – differentiating between good and bad challenges.

Me and my performance!

▶ What does your balance on the Performance Curve look like?

_____

_____

_____

_____

▶ Do you remember a time when you were performing at your optimum, when you felt good, in flow with life, motivated and stimulated but in balance? Describe below:

_____

_____

_____

_____

▶ **Do you know what conditions you need to perform well and feel good?**

_____

_____

_____

_____

➜ Locus of control

So who is responsible for my stress/happiness?

Locus of control

Take a look at the following statements and see if you agree or disagree with them:

	Agree	Disagree
• A stressful reaction is something you create in yourself		
• It is your perception of events, rather than the events themselves, which is the problem		
• Believing it is the events which are responsible keeps you a victim of your experience		
• You and no one else is responsible for your reactions – emotional, mental and physical		

You may have difficulty computing some of these statements, particularly when it comes to situations that you may perceive to be completely out of your control, such as ill health, climatic disaster, a car crash, poverty and many other adverse events.

There is no doubt that these are all extremely challenging situations.

We may not be able to stop some things happening (if we could the insurance companies would instantly go bust), but there may be circumstances after the event where we do have some influence over how we respond.

 **Exercise 29:**

Locus of control example

Think about a challenging event or situation you experienced:

▶ What happened?

_____

_____

_____

_____

_____

▶ What was out of your control?

_____

_____

_____

_____

_____

▶ **What was in your control?**

_____

_____

_____

_____

▶ **How did you respond?**

_____

_____

_____

_____

···

EXTERNAL/INTERNAL LOCUS OF CONTROL

There are some external factors which happen and we could predict or influence these with hindsight or mindful planning or attention.

Being alert to danger, but willing to take a chance is an everyday experience for most. E.g.

▶ Should I overtake now in traffic, should I react to this accusation, should I walk away from this relationship/job?

▶ Should I refuse this request for my time?

▶ Should I grasp this opportunity?

▶ Should I speak up at this meeting?

A more internal locus of control will increase your **sense of power** in making choices about how you respond to the conditions around you – this leads to more flexible thinking and less self-demands on fixed positions – e.g. 'I must please others at all costs!'

Summary

- ▶ We can choose our work/life balance and where we focus our energy.

- ▶ Stress and happiness can co-exist and may go up and down depending on our external and internal experience of life.

- ▶ Symptoms of stress and happiness can be measured by how positive we feel in relation to our thoughts, actions, physical self and emotional well-being.

- ▶ We can be over-stretched and under-stretched. Both can be stressful; balance is the key.

- ▶ We can feel more powerful if we recognize that we can control our responses to external or internal events.

My learnings from this chapter

_____

_____

_____

_____

_____

_____

Positive thoughts

_____

_____

_____

_____

_____

Where to next?

In the next chapter we will look at how personality impacts how we deal with stress.

Nature vs nurture

Nature vs nurture

As I watch my 18-month-old granddaughter Lily develop, I am filled with wonder as she moves through the different stages of development. Her first steps; mimicking our expressions – we laugh she laughs; the effort of forming her first words; how she copes when she bangs her head or falls over; how similar or dissimilar she might be to her parents and even her grandparents. I find myself wondering:

- How will she cope with life?

- Who will she take after?

- Who will she grow up to be?

- What will she be good at?

→ Stress and resilience

HOW MUCH CAN WE CHANGE?

What really interests me is how we can use knowledge about our personality, strengths, virtues, habits and behaviours to help us make choices.

It is a complex subject so forgive me if I simplify the subject to help answer these questions!

If we look at the inverse triangle below we can imagine that we are beings of many layers. The easiest layer to change is the 'top 'layer. When you are getting to know someone this is the safe information and topics which reveal very little about us like the weather. When on holiday there is a lot of discussion about the weather knowing you may not see the person(s) you are chatting with again so there seems little point in getting to know them at a deeper level. The more reason we have to invest in relationships the more we reveal about ourselves.

When it comes to changing behaviour we are more open to top layer changes as they may not touch the values we hold close to us. The deeper we go below the surface, the more challenging it is for us to change, especially when it comes to deeply held beliefs. There is an irony here as it is our beliefs which can either support us, or, if they are no longer useful, also sabotage us!

This is where we can do good work especially in becoming aware of our own traits and drivers. We can make assumptions that we can't change. Did you know that changing attitudes from those of a pessimist to optimist, for example, is very doable?

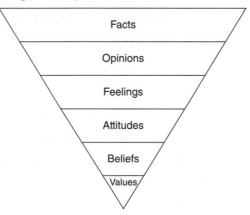

→ Personality theory

Questions about how much humans can adapt have been posed by many philosophers, scientists, academics, educationalists and psychologists, with many theories about what influences us most – **Nature** or **Nurture** – being explored, researched, debated and argued. In short most agree that roughly 50 per cent of our personality is influenced by heritability and 50 per cent by our environment.

There are many theories about personality traits but it is generally widely accepted that there are five core personality traits – traits being stable over time. Research over the last 50 years includes the work of D.W. Fiske (1949) and later Norman (1967), Smith (1967), Goldberg (1981) and McCrae and Costa (1987).

The **'Big Five Personality Traits'** are described as follows:

Openness	To new experiences
Conscientiousness	Being careful and self-disciplined
Extraversion	Being assertive and seeking out excitement
Agreeableness	A tendency towards being pleasant and accommodating/tough-mindedness
Neuroticism	Reflects emotional states

There are no wrongs or rights about where you are on this scale. Each of the five personality factors represents a continuum between two extremes.

For example, extraversion represents a continuum between extreme Extraversion and extreme Introversion.

Most people lie somewhere in between the two ends of each dimension.

If you wish to take a questionnaire about this the **NEO** (Personality Inventory) is a very good one to take – look it up on the Internet. See References at the end of this book for details.

 Exercise 30:

The five personality domains

You probably have a good idea about where you might be within these five domains and may want to give yourself a 'ball park' score on the continuum.

	V Low	Low	Ave	High	V High	
Openness Traditional	←				→	Ideas/novelty
Conscientiousness Disorganized	←				→	Well prepared
Extraversion Introverted	←			→		Gregarious
Agreeableness Competitive	←			→		Accommodating
Neuroticism Calm	←			→		Anxious

→ Developing talents

So what does this mean in terms of how we manage stress, develop resilience and even happiness?

Certainly some of our physical characteristics are clearly inherited and some vulnerability to disease and life expectancy can be linked to genetics.

Perhaps the more important question is about talents and strengths – what can we **choose** to develop? If so, what can help us become more resilient?

We can certainly develop these talents within a range and certainly much effort goes into nurturing our offspring to make the most of their talents. Picture parents and significant others shouting on Jimmy's sports day!

Natural talents

▶ What are your natural talents?

_____

_____

_____

▶ **What do YOU do to use your talents?**

_____

_____

_____

_____

_____

_____

→ Strengths and virtues

What is exciting to me in the world of coaching and developing potential is the degree of scope there is for developing what Seligman describes as our strengths and virtues regardless of our innate talents. These came out of research he undertook with Christopher Peterson in reading the basic writings of all the major religious and philosophical traditions in order to catalogue what each claimed were the virtues. He describes six virtues:

▶ Wisdom

▶ Courage

▶ Humanity

▶ Justice

▶ Temperance

▶ Transcendence

These are broken down in Seligman's book _Authentic Happiness_ (2002) as 24 strengths. These are likely to become traits if they are acted on consistently over a period of time.

Take a look at each of these in turn and next to those you can relate to record an example of when you have felt and acted on these strengths. Make some bullet points to remind you of examples of you demonstrating these strengths:

My Strength?	Examples
Wisdom 1. *Curiosity/interest in the world* 2. *Love of learning* 3. *Judgement /critical thinking/open-mindedness* 4. *Ingenuity /originality/practical intelligence* 5. *Social intelligence/personal intelligence /emotional intelligence* 6. *Perspective*	
Courage 7. *Valour and bravery* 8. *Perseverance/industry/diligence* 9. *Integrity/genuineness/honesty*	
Humanity and love 10. *Kindness and generosity* 11. *Loving and allowing oneself to be loved*	
Justice 12. *Citizenship/duty/teamwork/loyalty* 13. *Fairness and equity* 14. *Leadership*	
Temperance 15. *Self-control* 16. *Prudence/discretion/caution* 17. *Humility and modesty*	
Transcendence 18. *Appreciation of beauty and excellence* 19. *Gratitude* 20. *Hope/optimism/future-mindedness* 21. *Spirituality/sense of purpose/faith/religiousness* 22. *Forgiveness and mercy* 23. *Playful/sense of humour* 24. *Zest/ passion/enthusiasm*	

If you recognize all these strengths in yourself you are **amazing!** We aren't aiming for perfection or saintliness here though as that would just be too much pressure for anyone to handle!

However my suggestion is that you ask yourself the following questions:

Exercise 32:

Strengths and virtues

What are your top five?

This self-analysis may give you an idea about what Seligman calls your **top five signature strengths**. This may reinforce how you identify with yourself and what makes you and others feel good about what you do:

1 _____

2 _____

3 _____

4 _____

5 _____

What strengths would you like to develop?

1 _____

2 _____

3 _____

4 _____

5 _____

The great thing is that you **CAN** develop these strengths and they may support you in being more resilient and happier in your life.

⏱ *Exercise 33:*

Stepping into your strengths and virtues

Imagine if you were to step into these existing and desired strengths with more conviction.

▶ **How would you feel differently about yourself and others?**

_____

_____

_____

_____

▶ **How might others feel about you?**

_____

_____

_____

_____

Yourself!	Me about others!	Others about me!
I would feel more....	*How I might feel about others?*	*How others might feel about me?*

→ Personality and drivers

So far we can surmise that personality may be formed of some nature and some nurture, but may not be exactly sure which bits come from where.

In the attempts we make to fit in with society and be accepted we can develop **drivers**. Some are nurtured in us by significant others including organizations we work for. The term **drivers** describes some of the pressures that we feel make us do things in certain ways, e.g:

- ► Being perfect
- ► Being productive
- ► Being right
- ► Being liked
- ► Being loved
- ► Trying hard
- ► Being strong
- ► Going fast
- ► Being in control
- ► Being the best
- ► Demands for success
- ► Demands to stay positive and optimistic no matter what!
- ► ...and the list goes on – I'm exhausted already!

There is one big one missing here:

- ► The demands we place on ourselves to be **all things to everyone at all times!**

Exercise 34:

Demands I place on ME!

Add some of your own demands you place on yourself.

These may be things which contribute to you feeling **'squeezed'**.

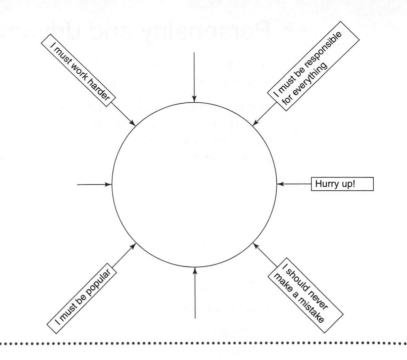

We could attribute these drivers to all sorts of psychological and humanistic models, e.g. **Maslow** or **Freudian** teachings but what matters is what we believe and then if we act on these beliefs whether it helps us or sabotages us.

 The impact can be felt at work and in our lives in general. I see these drivers in many leaders and professionals which place an intolerable pressure on individuals to perform. Organizations love them, but enlightened employers realize that if they want to retain their good people for longer they need to encourage a healthy work/life balance and well-being.

→ Personality and behaviour

TYPE A/TYPE B

There has been a good deal of research about personalities and those which appear to be resilient to stress. **Friedman** and **Rosenman** looked into the relationship between people's habitual ways of behaving and their associated risks of heart attacks. They came up with **high risk** which they called **Type A** and **low risk** which they called **Type B.**

Here is my interpretation of some of the Type A/B habits. Take a look at these behaviour patterns and tick those you recognize in yourself:

Exercise 35:

Type A personality?

Time management	✓/✗
Driven to achieve more	
Does more than one thing at a time	
Fast (hurry sickness)	
Impatient	
Over talks, finishes others' sentences	
Feels guilty relaxing	

Achieving	✓/✗
Aggressively striving	
Ignores feelings of others	
Highly competitive	
Achievement driven	

Relationships	✓/✗
High levels of hostility	
Resentful and suspicious of others	
Cynical, aggressive and hostile in relationships	
Very high energy	

You'll see that this behaviour models self-interest, ambition, and achievement as priorities, but others may get left behind, particularly if you are a leader of teams. In families this can cause conflict too! It's not all bad of course: **'fire in the belly'** gets us through difficulty and many competitive sports encourage these behaviours. But if we are out of balance, we can become a kind of cartoon caricature of ourselves. Over time it is also threatening to our health.

These behaviours may have their place in competitive sport, but in the 'real world', if extreme they are self-limiting.

This is where if you wish to improve well-being and 'achieve more with less effort', movement towards more Type B behaviours come in.

These are:

Type B personality?

Time management	✓/✗
Takes a longer view	
Realistic targets	
Trusts others to help	
Plans step by step but allows time for emergencies	
Manages others' demands	
Can constructively say no	
Doesn't feel guilty relaxing	
Work/life balance	

Achieving	✓/✗
Adding value more important than speed	
Can see the big picture/perspective	
Chooses where to place energy	
Maintains a sense of balance about demands and challenges	
Gets as much done in the long run	

Relationships	✓/✗
Easy-going, not hostile	
Win/win	
Collaborates	
Open-minded	
Engages others	

Type 'A' and 'B' personalities can be characterized by the children's fable the *Hare and the Tortoise* where the hare in his arrogance, lack of focus and last minute dash for the winning line is beaten by the slow, steady but clearly focused tortoise.

→ Life positions

The optimist, pessimist and realist

Achieving balance is a clear message in managing ourselves and our demands.

I mentioned pessimistic behaviours and how we might develop a more optimistic outlook which may in turn generate more positive emotions and happiness! However, being too optimistic can get us into trouble if we take too much on. Let's take a look at what a balance might look like:

THE OPTIMIST

The famous children's fictional adventure of Pollyanna (Eleanor H. Porter) reminds us of the optimism we can find in any situation. It is a story of an orphan girl who brings the 'glad game' and gladness to her guardian aunt in a downhearted New England town, until she is hit by a car and loses her spirit along with the use of her legs. The town consequently rallies and inspires her fight to recover resulting in her learning to walk again. Inspirational stories, heroic events in crises reinforce the human spirit to fight the good fight and keep going.

The optimistic approach can be heart-warming but could also be said to be excessive when faced with a specific set of circumstances without the necessary resources and support to be able to cope. Imagine being alone on a battlefield without any support against an army. Our super heroes and heroines in novels and movies would survive, no doubt, but in reality no amount of positive thinking is going to magic you out of that situation intact!

In modern life the extreme optimist takes on excessive demands without the equivalent appropriate resources, demands mostly self-inflicted and translated into 'I must prove myself here – I am infallible', 'I am superman/superwoman'.

This can of course catch us out in the longer term, when we place too many demands on ourselves and others.

THE PESSIMIST

In contrast the pessimist in the extreme can be like a wet rag, dampening the spirit in themselves and others. Casting doubt on the possibilities, finding reasons and excuses why something can't be done.

'When I was 15-years-old my platform boots were out of fashion and I decided I should cut off the platforms to make them funkier. I had a plan and plastic soles standing by to stick on but hit resistance when my Dad said I couldn't use his saw to perform the operation and it wouldn't work anyway (the pessimistic view). Being a teenager I snuck into the garage anyway and used the forbidden saw to perform the operation. The look on his face when I walked in with my newly formed funky boots was a picture! I think we learned a great deal about each other that day – I earned the title "leaping Lynne" and learned how laughter and not taking ourselves too seriously is a great tonic!'

On a more serious note of course sometimes we need to exercise caution in dangerous situations but the interpretation of what may be 'dangerous ' if overgeneralized, stops people from trying and believing in their own ability to achieve.

THE REALIST

I'm not suggesting that you should never be optimistic or even pessimistic but be mindful that if we do overgeneralize we can get ourselves into self-limiting situations.

Another option is **Realism**. This is a kind of balance and check between the two. The realist looks at the goals set and the resources available to achieve those goals. In the case of the funky boots, in my mind I was being realistic with an optimistic outlook – others may disagree which didn't really matter to me at the time.

There are times when it does and will matter however. When you are trying to manage or sell your time, manage relationships and expectations and influence others it is an important life skill; to accept and communicate what is humanly possible for your sake and for others and making choices about when, where and what you wish to focus your energy on.

Every New Year we can come up with new and exciting resolutions and can fail to achieve them due to the lack of realism. Having motivational and exciting goals is still possible if you are a realist, but the difference is you apply the practical grounding to make them happen.

I often see light bulbs go on when clients realize that committing to too many demands has led to much of the stress they feel. It sounds obvious but it's not, as we are conditioned to deliver and provide and strive – very powerful forces within us! At the other end of the scale believing that **'I will fail'** leads to a sense of powerlessness … I believe these attitudes greatly influence the issue of taking **responsibility** for our response to stress and **taking control** versus continuing to be a victim of our circumstances.

Exercise 37:

Where am I on the pessimist/realist/optimist scale?

▶ **Where is your habitual preference on this scale?**

Pessimist	Realist	Optimist

⊙ ⊙ ⊙

► If you imagine this scale as a kind of radio, then you can visualize yourself turning the volume up or down to suit different circumstances, e.g.

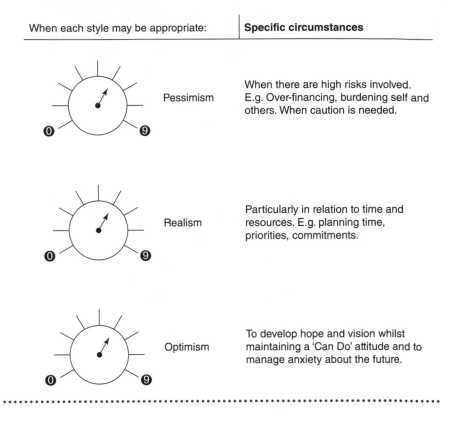

When each style may be appropriate:	Specific circumstances
Pessimism	When there are high risks involved. E.g. Over-financing, burdening self and others. When caution is needed.
Realism	Particularly in relation to time and resources. E.g. planning time, priorities, commitments.
Optimism	To develop hope and vision whilst maintaining a 'Can Do' attitude and to manage anxiety about the future.

Summary

► Whether you are born with natural resilience (nature) or develop it (nurture), what matters more are the choices you make.

► Drivers relate to how you feel you must behave and perform in life.

► Type A behaviour invites more stress. Movement to Type B behavioural choices encourages a more realistic life position.

► It is possible to develop realistic and optimistic approaches to life.

My learnings from this chapter

_____

_____

_____

_____

_____

_____

Positive thoughts

_____

_____

_____

_____

_____

_____

Where to next?

In the next chapter we will explore how you can become more aware of the impact of your thinking habits, and look at techniques for developing a positive mind-set.

Developing a positive mind-set

In this chapter we will cover:
▶ What is a positive mind-set?
▶ The benefits of a positive mind-set
▶ Positive and negative thinking habits
▶ Understanding emotions
▶ The TAPES model

The power of our thoughts

'Sometimes when people are under stress, they hate to think, and it's the time when they most need to think'

Bill Clinton

'A man is but the product of his thoughts. What he thinks, he becomes.'

Mahatma Gandhi

'Positive thinking will let you do everything better than negative thinking will.'

Zig Ziglar

'Thoughts aren't fact, so don't take them seriously.'

Ruby Wax

→ What is a positive mind-set?

We have already started to explore how a positive outlook on life can have direct impact on our happiness and how we get over setbacks.

A positive mind-set is a mind-set which supports you in:

▶ Feeling good;

▶ Achieving your goals;

▶ Focusing on what you can rather than can't do;

▶ Creates positive energy;

▶ Encourages flexible thinking;

▶ Helps you feel resourceful and powerful;

▶ Recognizes the reality of your situation;

▶ Develops inner and outer supporters!

THE ADVANTAGES OF A POSITIVE MIND-SET

An optimistic and appropriately realistic view of life and its challenges may have a direct effect on how empowered and resourceful we feel about overcoming obstacles. Other benefits of a positive outlook include:

▶ Improved sense of well-being and the chances of a longer life

▶ Lower blood pressure, stronger immune system

▶ Positive moods develop positive outcomes

▶ People like/love us more

▶ We have more open minds to possibilities

▶ We are more tolerant and able to manage setbacks

 *Exercise 38:*

The advantages of a positive mind-set

There may be some other advantages that you believe benefit you.

Make a note of them here...

_____

_____

_____

_____

_____

_____

_____

_____

· ·

One of the symptoms of depression is pessimistic thinking leading to a feeling of despair and hopelessness. Our thoughts can, through habit, become automatic and can influence whether we feel we have choice or are victims of our fate. Recovery from depression is inspired by hope together with support, improving health and learning strategies for well-being.

In sport, performance coaching is very much about getting athletes to get into the right mind-set. Tricks like turning your back on mistakes and moving onwards rather than dwelling on what went wrong have sustained many a Wimbledon finalist.

Most of us don't want to be Olympians but simply to enjoy the experience of life more and make the most of our opportunities. While we can borrow some psychology from sport the context of winning may be different to achieving more fulfilment and happiness in life.

One thing is clear and that is the way we think impacts how we feel, what we do and how we physically respond – it may not happen exactly in that order but this chapter is essentially about the power we all have to choose how we think and feel about situations and events and then enjoy an increased sense of well-being and better outcomes.

I would like to re-introduce you to a simple model for reframing/reflecting on your thoughts and whole self. The TAPES model embraces your whole self and gives you a process for making change happen and literally changing your mind-set.

→ The 'TAPES' model

Everything we do is influenced by how we think. Our thoughts have a direct impact on how we act, physically respond and feel about events around us.

Sometimes we make excessive demands upon ourselves like 'I must be perfect' or 'I must be in control'. We could reframe these thoughts to 'I will do my best 'and 'I will recognize what I can control and let go of the things I can't influence'. Ironically, once we take the demand out of the thought we manage the anxiety attached to the demand and performance goes up!

The 'TAPES' model is a model for reflecting on and developing a positive mind-set. The mnemonic 'TAPES' is a metaphor for questioning the **tapes** running through our heads like internal voices or **scripts** we are adhering to. Sometimes our negative thoughts sabotage us. Reframing our thoughts helps us think and act more positively and constructively about the situations we face which in turn helps us feel good!

It is as simple as ABC!

A. Identify your negative thoughts and responses to a stress trigger.

B. Reframe your thoughts to influence a more positive response to a stress trigger.

C. Embed your reframe into a plan for action!

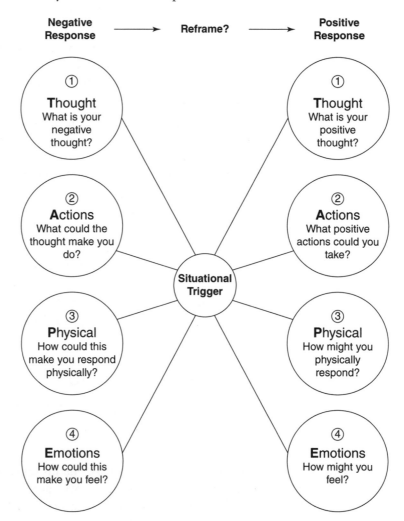

First let's get a feel for the context in which you might use the TAPES model.

EXAMPLE: A DAY IN THE OFFICE

Take 1: An observer's perspective

Juliana was known for having a short fuse so her colleagues walked on egg shells around her most of the time not knowing when she was likely to blow. The other day she entered a meeting with a black cloud hovering over her and a face like thunder – clearly something was bothering her. When it came to her turn her volcano erupted and she spewed expletives about why the tasks she had expected completion on hadn't been finished by others and how useless and inadequate several individuals were. The atmosphere was sickening – for her and for the rest of those present. She apologized later to the individuals she had insulted, but the damage was done and trust broken.

Take 2: Juliana's version of events

My day started badly. The alarm didn't go off and I was late for my train. The information desk was very unhelpful about alternative times and I was already seething and feeling victimized. This wasn't a great start to the day and I felt especially bad following the conversation I had last night with my partner about the mortgage rate going up and his lack of help around the house. 'What if I lose my job?' I thought. Also, there was no room to sit down on the train – typical!

Arriving in the office to a huge pile in my in-tray as well as 150 emails – all wanting an answer – I was told I had yet another meeting to attend! I muttered to myself as I entered the meeting room 'If everyone did their job in time I wouldn't be feeling like this – what a waste of ****** time!' The urge to vent was eventually too much and I told them what for! ... Later on at my desk I felt bad and thought 'I wish I hadn't reacted like that, now everyone hates me and I will definitely lose my job!'

Exercise 39:

A day in the office

▶ What were the 'triggers' for Juliana?

_____

_____

_____

▶ What thought patterns were the drivers behind her reactions?

_____

_____

_____

▶ What was the impact on her and on others?

_____

_____

_____

▶ How could she have managed her day differently?

_____

_____

_____

▶ How does this look in the TAPES model for Juliana?

_____

_____

_____

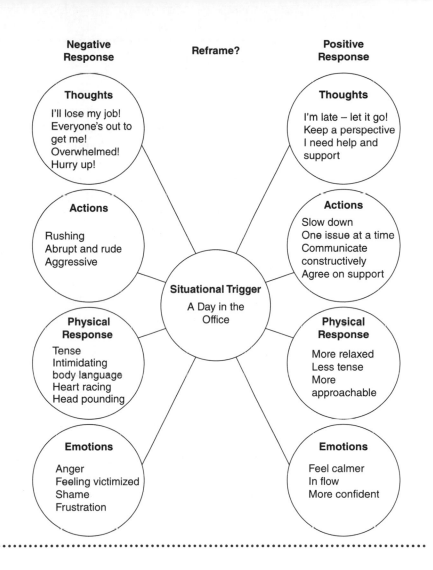

Negative Response

Thoughts

I'll lose my job!
Everyone's out to
get me!
Overwhelmed!
Hurry up!

Actions

Rushing
Abrupt and rude
Aggressive

Physical Response

Tense
Intimidating
body language
Heart racing
Head pounding

Emotions

Anger
Feeling victimized
Shame
Frustration

Reframe?

Situational Trigger

A Day in the Office

Positive Response

Thoughts

I'm late – let it go!
Keep a perspective
I need help and
support

Actions

Slow down
One issue at a time
Communicate
constructively
Agree on support

Physical Response

More relaxed
Less tense
More
approachable

Emotions

Feel calmer
In flow
More confident

We agonize, cogitate and have sleepless nights playing over the scenarios and negative consequences. At a deeper level we may fear loss, failure, humiliation, isolation and the list goes on – all black holes of the psyche. These internal voices can drive us to achieve, push us into high pressure zones and can be so habitual and automatic, that we can be blind to the impact on ourselves and others around us.

All this needs to be continually managed as the world and you are ever changing and like the weather are subject to storms and dry spells, so we need to monitor and regulate ourselves on a daily basis to make sure we maintain a balance. It means also that we take responsibility for what happens to us and the outcomes we are looking for. This can be a mind shift which can change your way of looking at life and empower you to do great things!

Juliana Take 3

It was a difficult message to take in that the mortgage rate had gone up especially at a time when finances were tight and jobs not 100 per cent secure. However Juliana reminded herself that catastrophizing might not help and she had survived for the last five years in her job so far. If she had to change her job she was extremely well qualified to look for another and she had a six-month notice in her contract. She immediately felt soothed by this thought and in a calm mood to discuss this and another issue with her partner. She told him she felt overwhelmed by the amount of housework she felt she had to do and how tired it was making her. He gave her a hug and they sat down and worked out a plan for who does what, and agreed to employ a cleaner to help with the housework – after all, while they were working it was a good investment. Again Juliana felt immediate relief and very inspired by the new window of time she and her partner were going to create together. The next day she knew she had a challenge with the amount of work coming in so asked her assistant to look at her workload and assess what was urgent and important. She would attempt to address the top three priorities that day only – anything else would be a bonus. She felt proud of herself for managing this and was feeling good about constructively contributing at the meeting and collaborating on the deadlines the team was working towards. The outcomes were positive and she felt a high level of energy and drive from her collaborators. This was turning out to be a great day.

An amazing turnaround for Juliana, with an example of two very different responses.

We can think negatively or positively in most situations. Here are some examples of negative and positive thinking patterns, some of which are illustrated in the Juliana example:

 **Exercise 40:**

Negative and positive thinking habits

Identify for yourself if you have these tendencies and make a note of specific circumstances when you have exhibited them.

Negative thinking patterns	Do you have this tendency?	Situation?
• Extreme demands on self and others		
• Catastrophizing – 'It will be a disaster!'		
• Magnification or minimization – blowing things out of proportion or minimizeing		
• All or nothing – sweeping generalizations – 'This always happens to me!'		
• Labelling – 'I'm a loser/he or she's a loser!'		
• Low tolerance of frustration – 'I can't stand it!'		
• Jumping to conclusions – personalizing 'He didn't smile at me so he must hate me'		
• Fortune telling – 'It will probably end up badly!'		
• Black and white thinking – 'I'm right, you're wrong!'		
• Musts/shoulds – criticizing self and others – creating guilt		
• Blame/denial – if things go wrong it's others' fault		

Positive thinking patterns	Do you have this tendency?	Situation?
• Realistic expectations		
• Flexible/adaptable thinking		
• Positive statements – identifies intent, can do/can't do		
• Focus on behaviour rather than personality		
• High tolerance of frustration, perspective taking and letting go of minor irritants		
• Open to possibilities and others' views		
• Curiosity – asks rather than assumes		

• Learning from mistakes and moving forward		
• Congratulating self/others		

→ Understanding your emotions

Understanding our emotions is a big part of self-management and self-awareness.

We don't always think about how we are feeling. Let's explore this.

 Exercise 41:

How am I feeling now?

Make a note of:

▶ How are you feeling right now?

_____

_____

_____

_____

▶ How were you feeling when you woke up this morning?

_____

_____

_____

_____

► How would you like to feel by the end of today?

_____

_____

_____

_____

Feelings give us real-time feedback about our values, beliefs, happiness, and unhappiness, and are our temperature gauge for life. We have feelings for a reason – in the early days to signal danger, build relationships and build communities. In modern times our feelings help us to keep safe and to manage boundaries between ourselves and the world, and give us the impetus to seek opportunities and propel us forward to survive and thrive.

Sometimes we go so fast that we forget to check our emotional temperature gauges or communicate how we are feeling to others. We probably spend more time tending to our cars than our own engines! This can push us out of balance and we can miss the danger signs when we are taking on too much or too little. Emotions are our feedback for happiness /discontent.

Exercise 42:

My emotions

How in touch with your emotions are you?

Consider this table and give yourself a 0–10 score depending on how frequently you experience this emotion.

0 = Never; 10 = Always:

	Emotional Responses	Score 0 to 10
Anger	*A strong feeling of displeasure, sometimes with feelings of hostility. A feeling of someone trespassing into your space.*	
Contempt	*The feeling of despising someone or having a lack of respect for something.*	

(continued)

	Emotional Responses	Score 0 to 10
Disgust	Active dislike for something caused by something highly distasteful.	
Embarrassment	The feeling of self-conscious distress, knowing that others are paying attention.	
Empathy	The ability to acknowledge what another person is feeling. Empathy can include understanding, sharing and responding to the feelings of someone else.	
Excitement	A feeling of heightened energy and expectation that often leads to joy. Excitement can come from anticipating or experiencing something enjoyable and it can also be part of feeling anxious or afraid.	
Fear	A feeling that comes from being scared of something, or when on heightened alert, expecting that something threatening is about to happen.	
Happiness	A feeling of contentment and overall well-being.	
Interest	A positive feeling when something or someone attracts attention and curiosity	
Pride	A feeling of pleasure that comes from believing or judging that something was done well.	
Sadness	A feeling of unhappiness that comes when something is lost or a goal is not met.	
Guilt	A feeling of remorse about what you should/could do.	
Despair	A loss of hope.	

One of the difficulties with emotions is working out what they mean.

You may have a general feeling of discontent, but not really know why. You just know you are in a bad mood!

Paying more attention to your emotions will help you regulate your moods. Often when we analyse our feelings, our moods can be influenced by something small. Like worrying about what a friend may be thinking about you. When you de-code what you're feeling, you then have access to forming a strategy to either doing something about it, or 'just let it go'.

Exercise 43:

Mood board

Creating a 'Mood Board' is one technique for analysing how you feel. Use the board to analyse your mood now and in the past 24 hours!

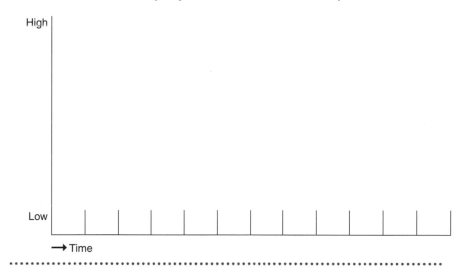

→ Open-mindedness

How open-minded are you?

An example of open-mindedness would be someone who is:

▶ Willing to learn

▶ Willing to think about different ways of doing things

▶ Not governed solely by conventional and traditional ways of doing things

▶ Able to see other possibilities

▶ Willing to try

▶ Able to see other perspectives

▶ Willing to reflect about themselves

▶ Willing to consider feedback and others' views

▶ Willing to make mistakes and learn from them

As the old saying goes 'you can lead a horse to water but you can't make it drink'.

We can be attached to beliefs around learning like:

▶ The old ways worked

▶ If it's not broken don't fix it!

▶ I'm too old to change now

▶ I like the way I am

▶ I need a reason to change

Strong values around change and whether change might be good or bad can influence whether we are close-minded or open-minded. It can also reflect independent strong-mindedness and resistance to outside influences resulting in oppositional, rebellious or resistant behaviour! To be fair there may be cases where an individual decides that there are some aspects of their lives with values which are non-negotiable and that is a choice as long as the consequences are understood!

 An example of this might be:

'I believe in the integrity of the scientific evidence and will fight with a passion and not compromise on these ethics.' (Perhaps the challenge here is not to change the value but to influence others effectively?)

 # Exercise 44:

Am I open-minded about change?

▶ **What are you open-minded about changing?**

_____

_____

_____

_____

_____

_____

_____

_____

► What are the non-negotiables?

_____

_____

_____

_____

_____

_____

_____

_____

_____

_____

_____

_____

→ Changing your mind-set

THE TAPES MODEL

Nelson Mandela worked out what he needed to do to manage himself in the environment which he had no control over. What he did have control over was how he responded to the environment with the thoughts, actions, physicality and emotions (TAPES) triggered by the stress of his imprisonment. No doubt his hope, compassion and vision had a profound impact on the choices he made.

You can use TAPES to address a particular issue you want to change your thinking about.

Exercise 45:

Reframing my issue

If you have an issue you would like to practise with, try it here:

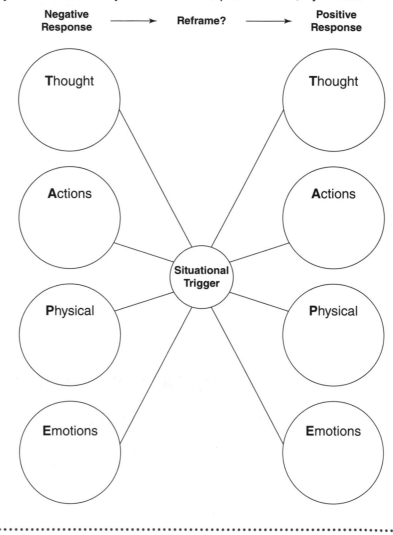

Negative Response → Reframe? → Positive Response

Thought

Actions

Situational Trigger

Physical

Emotions

Thought

Actions

Physical

Emotions

Summary

- ▶ Once you are aware of your thinking habits you can develop techniques for positive thinking.
- ▶ Our thoughts influence how we feel, act and physically respond.
- ▶ If we pay attention to our emotions we can regulate our moods.
- ▶ The TAPES model is a great tool for reframing negative to positive thinking and the associated responses.
- ▶ Being open to changing your mind increases your potential to lead a happier life!

My learnings from this chapter

_____

_____

_____

_____

_____

_____

Positive thoughts

_____

_____

_____

_____

_____

_____

Where to next?

 In the next chapter we will look at some strategies for managing performance anxiety.

Managing performance anxiety

In this chapter we will cover:
- ▶ What is performance anxiety?
- ▶ Understanding anxiety
- ▶ Managing the 'Inner Critics' and 'Inner Supporters'
- ▶ Using TAPES to reduce anxiety and enhance performance
- ▶ Visualizing success

Making choices and taking risks

'A little pony story'

I was reminded recently that making choices and assessing risk begins at a very early age. I overheard a conversation between a little girl and her riding instructor. The little girl was crying because she was about to mount her pony but was fearful because she had fallen off during the previous lesson. She was resisting any attempts from her mother to reassure her. The instructor responded like this:

'It was a shame you fell off before ... it happens sometimes and I can't guarantee that you won't ever fall off again, but that's what it's like riding ponies and hopefully the fun you have will outweigh the fear of getting on. But it's your choice whether you get on or not.'

I watched with fascination as within nano-seconds the little girl had computed the message, made a choice and was clambering on happily and had forgotten about her earlier bad experience. By the end of the lesson she had a huge grin on her face; I suspect not least because she was proud of herself and had proved to herself that she could do it. I too had a smile on my face for a long time after this heart-warming experience and was full of admiration for how skilfully and knowingly the instructor handled the situation.

The little girl realized she did have a choice even when the conditions were pretty risky and harsh and, empowered by her instructor, she decided to take responsibility for her actions. She realized that she did have some control in the situation. Her confidence grew that day!

→ What is performance anxiety?

We have all experienced anxiety at some point in our lives and a little anxiety can help us perform better and give us the edge in making the effort to overcome whatever challenge we face as best as we can.

The reasons why people may feel anxiety are wide and varied and the subject of many research projects. Some say personality has a big influence, others circumstances, and then there are the one-off situations, however big or small, which lodge in our memories and change the way we think or feel about things.

 I remember coaching someone who had a very quiet voice. He was very self-conscious about it and when I asked him if anything had happened to him which may have influenced this he sat for a few moments in very deep reflection. Slowly he responded with the following:

'I used to be in a choir and when invited to sing a solo in public was so filled with fear of hitting the wrong note that I seized up and could not perform. The choir leader was sympathetic afterwards but I felt ashamed and humiliated and that I had let the rest of the choir down. When I think about it that's when I lost my confidence in speaking up.'

His 'aha' moment (coach speak!) proved to be pivotal and the next day he arrived with a newly found voice!

This sounds a bit far-fetched but it is nevertheless true.

WHAT CAN YOU DO TO CHANGE?

What I would like to do in this chapter is to help you realize that you can develop your confidence in handling your anxiety by:

▶ Using courage and compassion – Understanding and embracing your anxiety compassionately;

- Developing a performance mind-set – Slowly and with the right support familiarizing yourself with new ways of thinking feeling and doing;
- Choice – Exercising your choice to change.
- Getting support and using some tools and techniques for reframing, relaxing and preparing for your challenge or goal which I will provide for you.

→ Understanding anxiety

 **Exercise 46:**

What causes you most anxiety?

Complete a Mind Map to capture this....

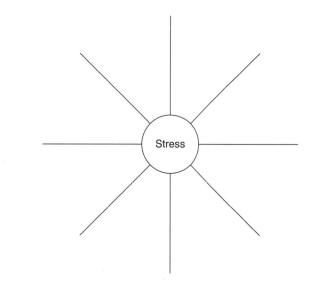

TYPICAL SITUATIONS REPORTED BY OTHERS MIGHT BE:

- on-the-job performance
- new job
- sitting an exam
- in relationships

- difficult conversations
- socializing
- presenting
- going to hospital
- meeting new people
- exposure to certain conditions
- situations perceived as high risk
- phobias
- giving up smoking /losing weight

... AND RESPONSES. SOMETIMES EXTREME OR IRRATIONAL FEARS RELATING TO:

- looking/feeling stupid
- losing credibility
- losing control
- being 'black listed'
- losing affection/love
- being embarrassed
- losing friends
- losing job

 It is important to recognize that we may all be vulnerable at different times in our lives and not to castigate yourself or allow others to stigmatize you about this, but to nurture yourself first back to health so that you can then start to make decisions about life and develop your own coping strategies.

 *Exercise 47:*

My fears

You'll notice that many of these examples of fear relate to the potential loss of something or other.

Do you have any other particular fears?

_____

_____

SOME DEFINITIONS

There can be confusion about different terms describing anxiety: some common types are defined below.

My experience of anxiety-excitement

Give yourself a score 0–10 if you have experienced any of the following. 0 = never; 10 = frequently

	Emotional Response	Score 0–10
Anxiety	This includes short-term or longer-term fears of perceived dangers. The effects of fight/flight/freeze if mild, can be helpful for gearing up for performance or a challenge. The effects may be more severe especially if prolonged. Poor diet, exhaustion, caffeine, excess sugar, stress and certain drugs can trigger anxiety.	
Panic attack	This is a sense of being overwhelmed by fear; pounding heart, sweating, shaking, feeling faint, breathing erratically, nausea, feeling out of control and powerless. It may feel like you are going mad or even dying. This all adds up to a terrifying experience. They tend to be short-lived – on average between 5 and 20 minutes. Sometimes people only ever experience a panic attack once in their lives, others more regularly. Breathing slowly and rhythmically is one of the best known antidotes as well as gradual exposure to the perceived danger, managed by a qualified therapist. Seeing a GP is advisable.	
GAD	Generalized Anxiety Disorder – is a kind of low-level generalized anxiety over a prolonged period. According to the National Health Service in the UK this affects about 1 in 20 adults with the highest prevalence in adults in their 20s, possibly reflecting a learning stage in developing strategies for coping. There are medications available to control this together with therapies and self-management as described in this workbook.	

	Emotional Response	Score 0–10
Phobias	Put simply, this is an irrational fear of something and the list of phobias beyond the commonly known ones such as arachnophobia, agoraphobia, and claustrophobia is endless. Hypnotherapy and Cognitive Behavioural Therapy are very effective in treating these disturbing fears, as is medical support if needed.	
Depression	Feeling persistently sad or hopeless for weeks or months. The severity can be wide ranging from a mild feeling of low spirit to feeling suicidal. Anxiety can be one of the symptoms as well as loss of appetite, and feeling tired and tearful. It is important to take the symptoms seriously and consult a doctor rather than try to 'pull yourself together', as over time the symptoms can lead to burnout or breakdown.	
Performance nerves	These are the butterflies, nervousness and shortness of breath we may experience before a challenge, e.g. performing a musical solo. In check, these can enhance performance.	
Excitement	This is the kind of high energy buzz and fizz we can feel when really looking forward to something. Very similar to performance nerves but positive emotional override can sometimes make us frenetic!	
In flow	This is a feeling of being lost in the moment, engaged totally in the experience, not aware of feelings or thoughts but more focused on what you are doing; losing the kind of self-consciousness which we might feel before we are immersed in an experience.	

So the range of anxieties and stimulation can be very wide.

→ Developing a performance mind-set

CREATING THE CONDITIONS TO PERFORM

New research from Harvard Business School found that getting excited – rather than relaxed – about the prospect of singing or speaking in public was a far more effective way to reduce performance anxiety.

I believe that when we manage our performance in general and all aspects of our life what we need to do is the following:

STEP 1: Soothe – soothe our negative anxieties: managing your negative or pessimistic thoughts, emotions and 'inner critics'.

STEP 2: Engage positive energy – turn our energies towards positive excitement and possibilities.

STEP 3: Centre – centre ourselves and create the conditions to perform. Visualize coping strategies and as we build confidence, develop conditions for success and a positive resourceful mind-set.

→ STEP 1: Soothe

What we are aiming to **soothe** is our negative thoughts and emotions.

We did cover some negative thinking patterns in Chapter 5 but here are some relating to:

ANXIETY

▶ Making sweeping statements like 'I am shy and therefore useless at connecting with others'

▶ Making judgements about self like 'I am my performance'

▶ Or predictions – 'It's not worth trying as I will only fail anyway'

▶ Catastrophizing – 'It's going to end in disaster!'

▶ Fixed thinking – 'I will never be able to conquer this' 'I will always be like this'

... AND EMOTIONS

▶ Demands for immediate gratification

▶ I can't stand it!

▶ Anger/blame towards others (projection)

▶ Withdrawal/avoidance

▶ Giving up trying

▶ Helplessness

▶ Self-flagellation

What we have captured are thoughts and feelings related to:

▶ Extreme/irrational expectations – relating to yourself and others

▶ All or nothing/extreme demands placed by you on yourself

At the heart of these fears if we work them back to source might be:

▶ 'Am I good enough?' (Imposter Syndrome)

▶ 'Am I loveable?'

▶ 'Am I in control?'

These thoughts might be sensitivities we have picked up from childhood. We create **scripts** which we use as our **rule book for life**, which may not now serve us and if left unchallenged can lead us down blind alleys or to judgements which really don't help us.

It never ceases to amaze me how many talented, intelligent clients can feel they aren't good enough, will be 'found out' even though they may have proved their worth time and time again. Part of the mind shift here is to help them to see themselves as others do and recognize the evidence of their achievements.

What we are looking for is balance:

Avoidance		Trying!!!		In at the deep end
Not trying enough. Learned helplessness.				Possibly landing in the Stress Zone!

Trying and doing our best is a reasonable self-expectation but progress should be one easy step at a time! 'In at the deep end' seems to work for some people who crave excitement but it may not be the best way to prepare for a challenge or manage self-development.

MANAGING THE INNER CRITICS

If you imagine we each have an inner voice you can then maybe stretch to thinking that at different times, depending on our scripts, we may have many voices! These voices in our heads, commenting on moment-to-moment experiences, are actually our thoughts and reflections of our scripts or tapes that we have running automatically. Sometimes they are supportive and nurturing which is great and these voices are our best friends and very welcome. Other times they undermine our confidence with their accusations, criticisms and bullying.

A wonderful mentor of mine, **Mary Hykel-Hunt,** calls these inner critics and supporters the **Committee of Selves**.

We may have a perfectionist voice which, like a nagging house guest, can really get on our nerves. Then there's the critical parent in us who keeps criticizing us for mistakes and inadequacies – very annoying!

Let's put some power back into you!

Imagine you are the owner/occupier of your house.

If you imagine you are the owner/occupier of your house what would it be like to have your guests constantly criticizing you! I suggest you treat the negative *inner critics* with the contempt they deserve!

INNER CRITICS CAN INCLUDE:

EXTERNAL DEMANDS

- ▶ Responsibility to others
- ▶ Pleasing others
- ▶ Working hard/long hours
- ▶ Competitiveness

INTERNAL DEMANDS

The inner critics:

- ▶ Pessimists
- ▶ Perfectionists
- ▶ Demanders – Immediate gratification

- ▶ Frustrated intolerants
- ▶ Procrastinators
- ▶ Avoiders
- ▶ Over-responsibles
- ▶ Under-responsibles
- ▶ And the list goes on …!

Exercise 49:

My other inner critics

Can you think of some others?

Take a look to see if you recognize any of these characters. Make a note of a couple of experiences beside each description if relevant – it helps to see these in context.

		Examples of:
Perfectionist:	Demands to be perfect no matter what the conditions. In early life stages it helps us pass exams and get good jobs but as life gets more complex it becomes impossible to perfect everything. Results in a super critical inner voice towards self and others and leads to avoidance of things we know we can't be perfect at. Creates performance anxiety! Selective perfectionism may be preferable.	
Demanders – Immediate gratification:	Demands that I must have it now and can't wait! Displays of childlike stamping of the foot and anger, even bullying others to give them what they want. Rushing around as if speed is most important. The expectation for immediate gratification causes stress and anxiety in self and others.	
Low frustration tolerance:	I can't stand it leads to intolerance and avoidance, e.g. queuing, things going wrong. Eruptions of emotion at small frustrations – sweating the small stuff.	

Procrastination/ Avoidance:	*This is linked with fear of consequences of not being successful, risk-taking, finding tasks overwhelming or boring – leads to last minute rushing and peaks of high anxiety.*	
Responsibility to others:	*When over responsible, feeling overwhelmed, overloaded and burdened, even resentful. When under responsible feeling guilty, lacking focus or bored. Unclear boundaries create confusion in communications.*	

… and there may be others!

→ Exercising choice!

Now imagine you have the power to veto or send them away, especially if they are bullying you or undermining you! What would that look like?

Draw in below the members who are present and identify the culprits you wish to eradicate – remember you are in charge!

Sometimes they may pop up unexpectedly, but they can still expect the same treatment from you – without mercy!

Yes your compassionate self is looking after you – hooray!

We can replace our inner critics with our inner nurturers:

New house guests – supporters, encouragers, empathizers, good challengers, courage, commitment …

… and all those virtues and strengths you have as your reinforcements!

→ STEP 2: Engage positive energy

→ How can we harness positive energy and stimulation?

One principle in managing anxiety is that excessively focusing on negatives can be a self-fulfilling prophecy and impact performance in a negative way. Equally if we are too ambitious or our expectations of ourselves and others are unrealistic, we enter the realms of fantasy land which can result in disappointment and a heightened sense of failure.

Exercise 50:

Harnessing your energy and stimulation.

Being clear about expectations is key.

Think of a performance challenge you have coming up and see if you can answer the following questions:

▶ **What is the specific performance you would like to improve?**

_____

_____

▶ **What are the desired results you want from the performance improvement?**

_____

_____

▶ **How would you currently rate your performance – on a scale from 0–10?**

_____

_____

▶ **Describe a recent typical example of this performance and the feedback you received.**

_____

_____

▶ What are the specific factors that hold back improvement in your performance?

_____

_____

▶ Are there any personal challenges that interfere with your performance?

_____

_____

▶ What do you think you could do to help improve your performance?

_____

_____

▶ Have you tried to improve your performance? If so, what happened?

_____

_____

▶ How would you know if your performance had improved? List observable and measurable changes.

_____

_____

_____

_____

▶ Other comments?

_____

_____

▶ What will you be thinking, doing physically and what emotions will you feel?

_____

_____

→ Using the TAPES model to develop a healthy mind-set

We have already concluded that everything we do is influenced by how we think. Use the next exercise to learn how you can manage your thoughts to reduce anxiety and improve your performance.

Exercise 51:

My performance challenge!

Complete the TAPES model by way of preparation for an upcoming challenge:

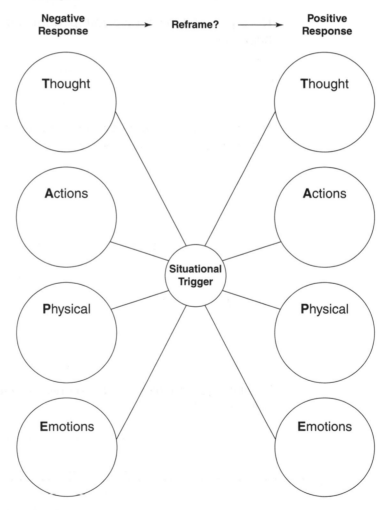

→ STEP 3: Centre

One of the problems in managing anxiety is that most of us have never learned how to use adrenaline to our **advantage**. Learning to welcome the excitement and rush of adrenaline and to **use** it positively as an energy source is beneficial. If we think too much about our performance we can get into **analysis paralysis** and if we allow our emotions to run away with us we can feel very out of control!

Centring and visualizing success

There are five steps, each specifically designed to move you progressively closer to right-brain calm, focus, and poise, and take you further away from left-brain fears, doubts and self-criticism.

- ▶ Find your physical centre – stand/sit, confidently feel your energy forming in your centre
- ▶ Visualize your goal
- ▶ Visualize yourself doing it positively (see – feel – hear) – visualize yourself coping with the possible challenges too!
- ▶ Breathe – long slow breaths in and out
- ▶ Use positive 'can do' affirmations – 'I will do my best to make this a great performance'

NB: don't use the word 'can't'. Describe only what you **can** do!

ANCHORS

In this context, an anchor is a reminder or reinforcement of the visual message using touch. It can take the form of an object you hold or touch, or pressure applied to a chosen part of your body, e.g. forefinger and thumb together.

You may like to use the next Exercise to prepare for an upcoming challenge.

Exercise 52:

Visualization

What is your goal?

Describe your goal or objective relating to a future challenge:

_____

_____

_____

_____

What is your anchor?

Choose an object or a form of touch that you will use immediately after you recollect your positive situation below:

_____

Past success

Pick a time when you had a positive/successful experience with either a similar or different situation:

_____

_____

Close your eyes and recollect:

▶ **What are you thinking?**

_____

_____

_____

▶ What are you doing?

_____

_____

_____

▶ What are you sensing (seeing, hearing, touch, smell, taste)?

_____

_____

_____

▶ How is your input or the result of your efforts received?

_____

_____

_____

▶ How do you feel?

_____

_____

_____

Anchor

Now anchor that good feeling with an object or touch. Breathe, relax and enjoy that feeling for 30 seconds.

When you are ready, open your eyes.

Future

Now using past positive experience as a resource, fast forward to your future successful self-facing your challenge. Close your eyes and imagine.

▶ What are you thinking?

_____

_____

_____

▶ What are you doing?

_____

_____

_____

▶ What are you sensing?

_____

_____

_____

▶ How is your input or the results of your efforts received?

_____

_____

_____

▶ How do you feel?

_____

_____

_____

Anchor

Anchor that good feeling and enjoy it for 30 seconds.

Open your eyes and release your anchor!

Summary

The techniques for improving performance and feeling good about yourself in the process, involve:

- ▶ Courage and compassion.
- ▶ Developing a performance mind-set.
- ▶ Exercising choice.
- ▶ Knowing we can all experience performance anxiety.
- ▶ Understanding that anxiety can range in intensity, with some positive and some negative outcomes.
- ▶ Soothing to engage positive energy and centre ourselves.
- ▶ Using TAPES and visualization as useful performance tools.
- ▶ Managing our inner critics and nurturing our inner supporters.
- ▶ Taking the demand out of our thinking so that anxiety goes down and performance goes up!

The TAPES Model and visualization techniques are very powerful in helping you get into a mind-set and centred position which supports you. Having realistic coping strategies will increase your confidence, and, with practice over time, will reinforce the value of excellence rather than perfectionism!

My learnings from this chapter

_____

_____

_____

_____

_____

_____

Positive thoughts

_____

_____

_____

_____

_____

Where to next?

In the next chapter we will be reflecting on life events and managing major personal change.

7 Navigating life events

In this chapter we will cover:

▶ Life events and how they can affect us
  ▷ Coping with change
  ▷ The STOP model
▶ Self-managing life events

'A shock!'

Simon had been working on the production line for a manufacturing company for 20 years. He was considered 'the expert' in the field of project management. The company had suffered post-recession as a result of decreasing sales of their main product line.

Simon was called in to see the boss. He was told that for all those reasons there was no longer a job for him. The news hit him like a bus. His world exploded and the shock sent him spiralling into panic and denial. This couldn't be happening? Surely it's a mistake? His world changed in an instant. He sat with his boss for an hour desperately trying to renegotiate and recover the world he knew. The boss kept repeating the message that this was really going to happen. The reality emerged through the red mist and he sat back defeated – the consequences spinning around in his head.

That evening he had to tell his wife the news; it was not easy to handle her shock when he too was still in shock. They talked for many hours and then his wife stopped and slowly reflected:

'Simon, have you ever stopped to think that this situation could be the making of us?'

Simon felt his first ray of hope as he absorbed the wisdom of her words.

→ Life's ups and downs

One example of a shock is redundancy. Some may accept this news with delight especially if accompanied by a good package. Others may feel their worlds collapsing.

This chapter is an exploration of how to handle life events and transition personal change. We will be looking at the impact of life events as triggers and tools for self-management.

When I think about my life, I have no regrets. This is because the down times put me in touch with my authentic and creative self and the up times gave me happy memories to look back on. The sum total providing a rich tapestry for weaving resources and the excitement to carry on! I know some may say they don't experience highs and lows, more of a steady state. Well this is OK too isn't it? We are **all** different!

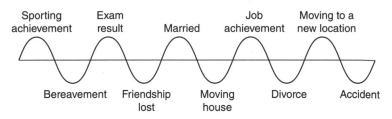

Life can be tough sometimes, it can be brilliant too. It is normal to have ups and downs, ebbs and flows as we navigate our way through. Many of the external events are out of our control but how we respond to them is within our control. We can acquire the most profound life lessons and develop lifelong coping strategies when we are at our lowest and as the saying goes:

> *'That which does not kill us makes us stronger!'*
>
> Friedrich Nietzsche, German Philosopher.

→ Transitioning change

As human beings we can look for certainty as it represents safety. If things stay the same at least we know where we are, who we are and what to expect. Each time we face change we go through a kind of transition process which most of the time may be invisible but results in us moving from endings to new beginnings, in real terms but also psychologically, emotionally and physically.

The stages we go through when we experience change, positive or negative, may vary from person to person. The psychiatrist Elisabeth Kubler-Ross identified transition stages resulting from her work on personal transition in grief and bereavement. This model was further developed by John Fisher (among many others).

Here is my take on this:

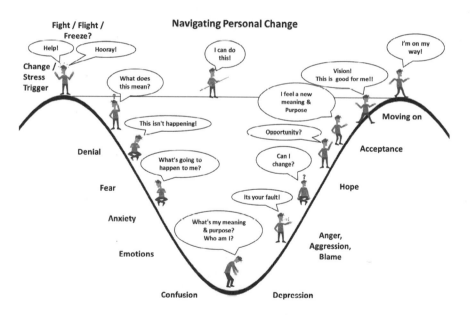

Sometimes when change occurs we lose our sense of who we are. We feel confused, depressed and our meaning and purpose can be shattered. Then if at the lowest ebb we take care of our health we can gradually piece together sense and meaning into our lives and see a way forward again.

I must add that some people love change and move from endings to new beginnings rubbing their hands with glee. However, this is not necessarily an aspiration as there may be a gap in self-reflection, and we may miss the insights we can gain from stepping back mindfully and considering the impact change is having on us and others.

→ Life events

Here are some typical life events:

 **Exercise 53:**

Life events

Tick those which you are experiencing **now** as a kind of snapshot of your life **now**. Indicate '+' for positive and '−' for negative:

Loss	+ −	Habits	+ −	Life Stages	+ −
• Death of spouse		• Change in habits		• End/beginning of school/college/ University	
• Divorce		• Sleeping		• Retirement	
• Separation		• Eating			
• Prison		• Exercise			
• Death of a close family member					
• Son/daughter leaving home					

Work	+ –	Critical Incidents	+ –	Relationships	+ –
• Business readjustments		• Personal injury or illness		• Trouble with in-laws	
• Job loss		• Living arrangements/ conditions		• Changes in social/home life	
• Change in role/ responsibilities		• Marriage		• Family get-togethers	
• Different line of work		• Change in health		• Arguments with spouse	
• Spouse stopping or starting work		• Family member			
• Boss trouble		• Pregnancy			
• Working hours/ conditions		• Sex. difficulties			
		• New family member			
		• Outstanding achievement			
		• Pressure points – holidays/Christmas			
Finance					+ –
Financial change					
• Large mortgage loan					
• Foreclosure on loans/ mortgage					

The next exercise is more specifically related to work sources of satisfaction/dissatisfaction.

Exercise 54:

Sources of job satisfaction/dissatisfaction

Now that you have analysed your life in general, take a look at these work conditions and tick one of these boxes ranging from 'Not Satisfied' to 'Extremely Satisfied' to indicate your current satisfaction level:

The organization	Not satisfied at all	Somewhat satisfied	Satisfied	Very satisfied	Extremely satisfied
Consultation and information sharing?					
Policies/Ethics?					
Expectations?					
Meaning and purpose?					
Congruence with my values?					

My power to Influence	Not satisfied at all	Somewhat satisfied	Satisfied	Very satisfied	Extremely satisfied
Responsibility					
Authenticity					
Control					
Accountability					
Change					
Meaning and purpose					

Working conditions	Not satisfied at all	Somewhat satisfied	Satisfied	Very satisfied	Extremely satisfied
Motivating atmosphere?					
Workload?					
Social support?					
Work/life balance?					
Health and well-being?					
Physical working conditions?					
Travel					
Job security					

Career development	Not satisfied at all	Somewhat satisfied	Satisfied	Very satisfied	Extremely satisfied
Opportunities to progress?					
Coaching/Mentoring/Support/Training?					
Learning 'on the job'?					
Recognizing my strengths/potential					

Relationships	Not satisfied at all	Somewhat satisfied	Satisfied	Very satisfied	Extremely satisfied
With the boss?					
Colleagues?					
People who report to me?					
Others?					

My role	Not satisfied at all	Somewhat satisfied	Satisfied	Very satisfied	Extremely satisfied
Meaning and purpose?					
Role/structure?					
Vision/goals?					
Expectations?					
Involvement in decision making?					
Recognition for my achievements?					

→ The cumulative effect

If we only experienced one challenge at a time it would be easier to cope and manage, but real life doesn't work like that does it?

What can tip the balance is when we have to deal with one challenge after another like a hillock that builds into a mountain. Suddenly everything can seem completely overwhelming and the mountain collapses. We can mindfully manage this potential build up by continuously:

▶ Identifying and compartmentalizing issues as they arise.

▶ Dealing with unresolved issues, one at a time.

→ Your life's ups and downs

If you think about your life's ups and downs, I wonder what emerges.

Let's try to recall some you feel comfortable about by capturing some of the highs and lows or even constants in your life, over your lifetime.

Plot your lifeline on the chart below with the highs and lows you have experienced and note by each significant event, the people or experiences which led you to viewing the experience as you did. This can be a very powerful exercise as it evokes powerful memories and possible emotions about what happened in the past – if you feel you would like some support from someone you trust through this exercise please go ahead; if you don't want to look back skip this exercise and move on to the next paragraph.

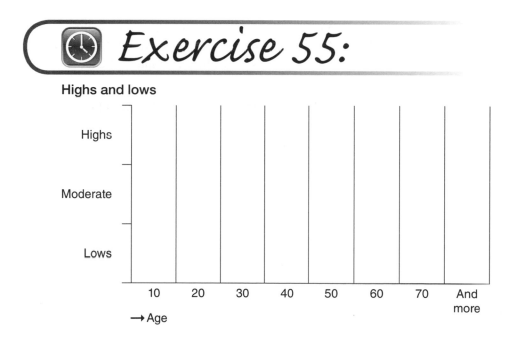

▶ What emerges as important influences in your life?

_____

_____

_____

▶ How did you navigate your way through these changes?

_____

_____

_____

▶ What positive lessons about yourself can you take from the way you handled these changes?

_____

_____

_____

 You may feel you could have done things differently and this may be learning in itself, but remember you did your best at the time. It is our life's learnings which help us build resilience not the events themselves!

→ Navigating life events

So changes may be good or bad depending on how we perceive what we can do to navigate them. These may relate to some of those events already identified above. For example:

▶ Loss /grief/change
▶ Critical incidents
▶ Work
▶ Finance
▶ Relationships

→ STOP!

I would like to introduce you to a very simple model which is an easy-to-remember process to guide you through life events. 'STOP' stands for:

Support – take time to reflect on:

- ▶ Support needed?
- ▶ Health/well-being?
- ▶ Impact on family, others?

Tapes:

- ▶ Impact on me?
- ▶ Responses to the event positive/negative?
- ▶ Reframing thoughts to support myself?

Options and Opportunities for:

- ▶ Action?
- ▶ Non action?

Plan·

- ▶ Prioritize
- ▶ Gain perspective for the way forward

Typically when we are under pressure or in shock, we may keep moving, shutdown, or carry on in denial – there are many other individual reactions. 'STOP' is a process for coming to our senses and viewing the territory with mindfulness, courage and compassion.

→ Loss/grief/change

Everyone responds differently to loss and change. Some people withdraw. Some talk to everyone, but the important thing to remember is to choose a path or strategy which suits you.

Social support is known to be a number one influencer in helping us overcome difficulty, especially for those who are close to you. Sometimes the physical effect of shock can shut you down (freeze response) from others or we can leave them behind (fight/flight). When we are in shock we get tunnel vision and self-interest takes over. We may be in no mood to support others, but we can allow others to help us. Being stoic and strong may or may not serve us at these times, so keep a careful eye on **you**.

Letting emotions out is a kind of catharsis and necessary for recovery. There are relationships, grief and loss counsellors out there for those experiencing extreme loss if you need it and it can be very helpful to get you in touch with yourself and come to terms with the loss.

There are some losses which take a great deal of support and recovery time to get over. Day by day and step by step. Loss of a loved one can involve much sadness, anger and confusion, as well as some celebration of the good memories and cherished moments.

I'm not suggesting you only feel positive or ignore your feelings of loss or sadness, but there are some coping mechanisms which can sabotage us. For example, withdrawal, denial, blame and negative coping habits like drink, drugs, etc.

At times like this it may be helpful to:

Remember STOP!

- ▶ Support
- ▶ TAPES
- ▶ Options
- ▶ Plan/perspective

Let me illustrate this process together with TAPES in relation to **Simon's story**.

EXAMPLE – SIMON'S REDUNDANCY

Support

Simon's news about his redundancy was an emotional rollercoaster for him and his wife.

Simon's main support was his wife and their soul-searching together gave them the support they needed to see things from a different perspective.

TAPES

Remember TAPES involves thinking about the questions which Simon explored with his wife:

1 What is the impact on me/us?

2 How am I/we responding to the event: positively/negatively?

3 What can I do to reframe my thoughts to support myself /my wife?

Options

▶ Action(s)

▶ Non action?

Just taking time out to think about the options for handling the situation can be positive in itself. There may be decisions to make, things to take care of, and short-term actions to put in place.

Plan

▶ Priorities

▶ Perspective for the way forward

Having a plan can be a big relief. You may not be able to change the circumstances or even wish to change them, but creating a structure is a good way of helping us to feel safe and to get some direction for the way forwards. Get some support and help in formulating a plan.

→ Simon's redundancy – TAPES

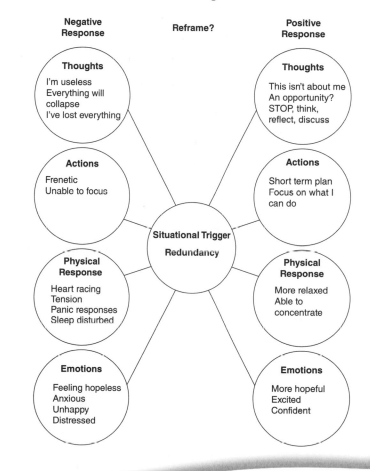

Exercise 56:

Critical incidents

Identify a critical incident which you are dealing with now, have done recently or anticipate coming up in the future.

Work through the STOP and TAPES models below to reflect and learn from:

Support

- ▶ Support needed?
- ▶ Health/well-being?
- ▶ Impact on family, others?

TAPES:

- ▶ Impact on me?
- ▶ Responses to the event positive/negative?
- ▶ Reframing thoughts to support you?
- ▶ Use the template following this checklist.

Options:

- ▶ Action?
- ▶ Non action?

Plan:

- ▶ Priorities?
- ▶ Gain perspective for the way forward?

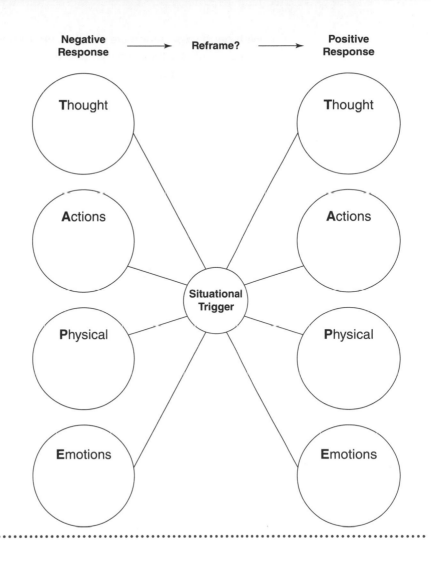

Negative Response → Reframe? → Positive Response

Thought

Actions

Physical

Emotions

Situational Trigger

Thought

Actions

Physical

Emotions

Summary

▶ Life can be challenging and we can navigate our way through events when we learn and apply our learning to those experiences.

▶ 'STOP' and 'TAPES' are models which encourage learning and provide a process for thinking flexibly about what we can do to ease the path and deal with change as constructively as we can.

▶ Change can bring opportunities too, it is the phase of loss and uncertainty which disturbs us most and we can feel like we have lost our sense of meaning and purpose at times.

▶ With each experience we survive, we generate new coping tools and strengths which we can use as resources in readiness for the next challenge!!

My learnings from this chapter

_____

_____

_____

_____

_____

Positive thoughts

_____

_____

_____

_____

_____

Where to next?

In the next chapter we will look at strategies for organizing your time and where you wish to focus your energy.

Organizing your time

In this chapter we will cover:
- ▶ How you spend your spare time
- ▶ Your time-related values
- ▶ Past, present and future focus
- ▶ Your style of time-management
- ▶ Managing demands and expectations
- ▶ Strategies for managing your time

Example – Jan's busy life

Jan was always busy. With a demanding marketing job, her grandson living with her and a long commute, she often arrived home from work frazzled and exhausted.

Nine times out of ten she walked into chaos at home. Her husband Nick seemed to be coping well at work, but he rarely took the initiative to tidy up or offer to help. She had really resented that he had not been more supportive in the past and an 'affair' he had had nearly split them up. The demands of cooking dinner, washing up and getting ready for the next day wiped her out. The mornings were frantic. When everything went according to plan it was bearable, but if the train was late or she needed to stay at the office late it felt to her like there was a conspiracy to sabotage her life! She often felt like her blood pressure was rising and her head pounding. She had a creative job and liked spontaneity and to be supportive of others.

Pleasing others, trying to be perfect – her inner critics were having a 'field day'.

She was a giver of the world and her emotional tanks were nearly empty.

→ Time is value loaded

How we spend our time is a very powerful reflection of what we value in life and these two are often at odds. Jan works hard to support her family but deep down her greatest desire is to have more time with them in a less pressurized environment, and some time for her to relax.

We spend our time on all kinds of activities for all kinds of reasons and mostly doing our best to survive and negotiate the challenges and demands which come our way. The mindful organizer is able to step back and see themselves; as observers of their own habits and behaviours they are able to self-correct and even avoid pressure points with clever foresight. However, we can't control everything and we are all only human and often under pressure the default button kicks in and we can become reactionary. We can step up to the pressure by working harder, longer, retreat into our own worlds and become angry, irritated and blaming others for our predicament and feel victimized. This affects our relationships and we can feel saturated by the demands of life.

Financial security, material satisfaction, desire to succeed and maintaining the things we have in life if out of balance, can drive us to 'Type A' behaviour and spoil the experience of life driven by what we have to do to acquire and maintain those things in the first place. The business of **having** and **doing** overtakes the business of **being**. The fear of losing the things we've worked for can create a kind of performance anxiety at work which then adds to the pressure.

Clearly it's not all bad; there is much joy to be had from balancing your life with the right level of challenges, stimulation and achieving your goals.

The theme for this workbook is managing our lives with mindful self-compassion, planning and self-awareness with the right tools and processes to support us.

Exercise 57:

What are your values about time? (Part 1)

Our values about time 'I must be productive 100% of the time' or 'hurry up' influence how we manage our time. For example, they create energy like fuel to a car. They are also drivers that make us 'head off' in a particular direction.

What are your values about time?

Note each influence and attribute a portion of 100% for each below to indicate the strength of each value:

I Must...	%	I Should...	%

Exercise 58:

What are your values about time? (Part 2)

Now by substituting the word 'Must' or 'Should' with 'Choose' in the preceding table, how does this change your perspective about your values on time?

→ Past, present and future

Where do you spend most of your time?

Where do you spend most of your time? Attribute a percentage in the table below. This is the time you spend thinking about doing things relating to the past, present or future.

Past	Present	Future	Total

This is a strange question but your answers could give you some great insights.

Exercise 60:

The past

Think about the time you spend either thinking or doing things relating to the past.

▶ What are those things?

_____

_____

_____

▶ What negative or positive feelings do you have about these thoughts or things?

_____

_____

_____

▶ How does this impact you and your time?

_____

_____

_____

▶ What benefit do you gain from investing your time in these past issues?

_____

_____

_____

▶ What are the disadvantages of investing your time in these issues?

_____

_____

_____

	Past issue	Negative feelings	Positive feelings	Impact on my time?	Benefits	Disadvantages
1.						
2.						
3.						
4.						
5.						

LIVING IN THE PAST

Sometimes we find it difficult to let go of our past. While happy memories are a great tonic, dwelling on past negative experiences and thoughts can keep us stuck, making it difficult to enjoy the present or plan for the future.

We can equally live vicariously through past memories and better times which sometimes can appear rosier in the mists of time. One of my dreams was to have a farm, based on very happy childhood memories of wonderful holidays on a farm, but when I finally researched and visited the real possibility of making it happen I realized I'd moved on in my needs and the prospect was nowhere near as romantic and attractive through adult eyes. We can trick ourselves into believing that times will never get better than they were and this can block the scope of exploration for new and interesting experiences for the future.

Past losses and regrets can destabilize us if unresolved and we can waste hours agonizing and persecuting ourselves and others.

Looking for ways to achieve closure secures the possibility of spending your time on more creative pursuits. This may involve some forgiveness of yourself or others and acceptance that you survived and cannot change the past.

That is not to say that you forget, but just choose to move on.

Exercise 61:

Closure and celebrating achievements

Capture some ideas for action/closure or even celebrating past achievements.

Let go or release	Treasured moments and positive moments from the past

In Jan's case, she had to stop this perpetual feeling of being a 'hamster in a wheel'. She discussed it with her husband and he asked her one big question … 'Why do you feel you have to take all of this on?'

Exercise 62:

The future

Think about the time you spend either thinking or doing things relating to the future.

▶ **What are those things?**

_____

_____

_____

▶ **What negative or positive feelings do you have when you think about or act on those things?**

_____

_____

_____

▶ **How does this impact you and your time?**

_____

_____

_____

▶ **What benefits do you get for focusing your energy on those challenges?**

_____

_____

_____

Thinking about the future?

	Issue/Worry?	Negative Feelings	Positive Feelings	Impact on Time?	Benefits	Disadvantages
1.						
2.						
3.						
4.						
5.						

It is necessary for us to apply some foresight and planning to life. Concern and application keeps us from avoiding danger and helps us seek out opportunities. However, if we spend an excessive amount of time worrying about the future it can create anxiety and stress and even keep us awake at night. At worst we can spend our days chasing the future, competing with the clock in order to meet deadlines and goals, rushing here, rushing there on a mission to beat time. Those around us have the experience of you that you are not really present but in a state of readiness to move on that you are not able to hear or listen to them and irritated by any attempt to bring you into the present. Sometimes the environment reinforces this. Work ethics to be super-productive, super-fast with super efficiency creates this superman/superwoman mentality which is impossible to sustain over the long term. The word **super** seems to supersede many of the demands of the modern world!

Reality check! Only we can protect ourselves from these demands and if we choose to run not walk then we suffer the consequences. Having a sense of balance and what is realistically possible in the 24/7 you have available to you is a great step in the right direction. Like diets, if you cheat with yourself around time and what is humanly possible you only cheat yourself and you bear the impact!

Enlightened self-interest, courage to manage yourself and others with compassion is the way to go!

Capture some ideas for achieving more by giving realistic answers to the following questions.

Exercise 63:

The present

Think about the time you spend either thinking or doing things relating to the present.

▶ **What are those things?**

_____

_____

_____

_____

▶ **What negative or positive feelings do you have related to those things?**

_____

_____

_____

_____

▶ **How does this impact you and your time?**

_____

_____

_____

_____

▶ **What are the benefits of thinking or doing these things?**

_____

_____

_____

_____

▶ **What are the disadvantages of thinking or doing these things?**

_____

_____

_____

_____

Being present is not necessarily the goal but more a state of being and we need to do some planning for the future in order to feel safe and make things happen. However mindful planning can help us be present even when we are in 'planning' mode, allowing sufficient and realistic time to apply ourselves to the activities in hand and movement from one activity to another so that we can feel a sense of enjoyment of the moments and the natural **ups** and **downs** of life.

We only have the present. The past is gone and the future is fantasy. When we are in the present we can place our energies into our strengths and virtues and concentrate on the business of being and living. We can feel more 'in flow' with life and play to our meaning and purpose.

Being present in challenges/activities	Negative feelings	Positive feelings	How important is your time?	Benefits	Disadvantages

→ What's your style relating to how you plan?

We are unique as human beings. Along the way we have picked up habits and values, some of which are helpful, some of which are definitely unhelpful! Often our strengths and desires if underplayed or overplayed can become our weaknesses. These can influence our ability to organize ourselves and others effectively. Here are some examples of styles relating to self-organization.

What's my style?

Tick those most relevant to your style.

The Butterfly	Flits here and there 'that's interesting' and 'I think I'll do something else now – I'm bored with that'. The internet may be Googled out by this person and the experience of this person juggling multiple tasks, not necessarily in the right order is noticed by others.	
The Reactor	Responds to any demands as they arise and tries to please and satisfy all requests preferably immediately. Consequently any planned activities disappear out of the window.	
The Analyst	Analysing this and that just in case the information is needed. Super tables and super data. Masses of information at the fingertips and long hours perfecting and getting it right. Sometimes deadlines must be extended to allow for all the research and rightness.	
The Flexible Planner	Keep things flexible and open at all costs so depending on where the mood takes me: I can duck and dive, rock and roll, have fun and keep my time within my control. Hopefully everyone else knows what they are doing.	
The People Pleaser	Cares and nurtures others' needs to the point where others' emotional tanks may be full and theirs empty. At work they have a long queue of people at the open door. Always available to listen. Drops everything if anyone is in trouble even if they don't want any help.	

The Producer	Productivity is more important than the experience of life. Getting results is what it's all about. Missing deadlines is not acceptable and causes extreme stress even if the deadlines are self-imposed.
The Controller	Keeping things in control and ordered helps keep risk to a minimum. It avoids possible mistakes (in my eyes), helps me get things done in my way and keeps everyone safe, even if they are perfectly capable of looking after themselves.

This is a deliberately humorous look at traits and outcomes. If we are honest with ourselves, some of these may reflect just how we react! Jot a few notes against these styles to remind yourself of your preferred style.

If none of these fit, describe your style here:

_____

_____

_____

_____

→ # Self-expectations/expectations from others

Thinking about where you put you energy and how you respond to demands may give you a feeling of coping or feeling overwhelmed. When we are in automatic pilot mode we just respond. We can then become saturated and over time feel quite unwell. Equally, we can be bored and uninspired.

Exercise 65:

Demands on your time

Using the model below make a note of demands for your time which you experience:

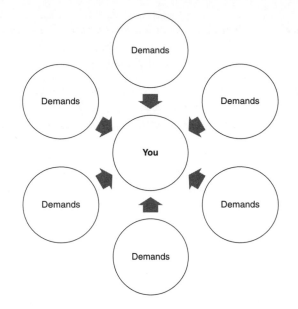

▶ How do you feel in response to those demands?

_____

_____

_____

▶ What is your cognitive reasoning for accepting those demands?

_____

_____

_____

▶ How does this make you feel physically?

_____

_____

_____

▶ How do you behave in response to those demands?

_____

_____

_____

MODEL OF CONTROLLED DEMANDS

If you were to reverse the process and instead of these demands controlling you, you controlled them – what would the picture look like?

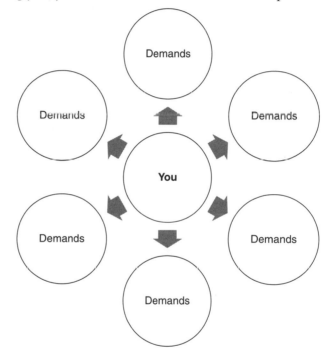

→ Taking control

Taking control may not be about trying to control everything; this would be an impossible and not necessarily desirable goal. Sometimes it's about letting go too.

Jan knew she had to change her ways, she had reached her toleration point and things had to change.

She put a plan together which would create a more supportive environment for her and her family and also allow her to achieve at work. She agreed with her husband what she was able to do in the house and with her grandson and what her husband would take on. He also agreed to attend some mediation counselling sessions to help her let go of the past.

At work she decided to leave earlier more regularly and be less responsive to requests which required immediate gratification. By planning and educating others about her availability she had more of a chance of managing her workload and setting some boundaries around finishing on time.

She employed a childminder to take her grandson to school and to be on call should any difficulties occur at the other end of the day. Jan felt lighter.

Jan felt relieved and her more realistic schedule improved her mood and communications. She scheduled some fun and much-needed family time into her diary.

Life was definitely worth living again.

Exercise 66:

Managing time strategies

Jan asked herself the following questions in relation to her work and her home life.

Record your answers in the circles as appropriate, they may reveal some interesting insights!

▶ What is most important to me?
▶ How can I add most value?

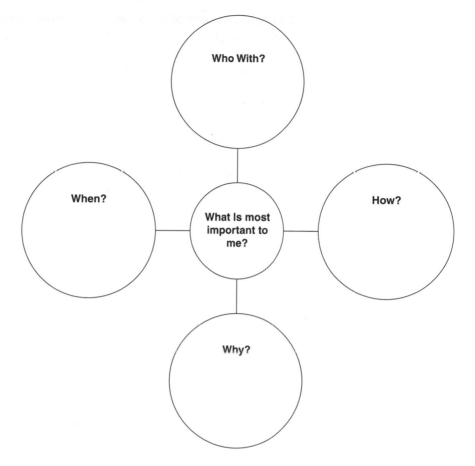

► Biorhythms – When am I most effective?

Daytime Energy Flow		
	am	pm
High		
Low		

► Biorhythms are unique for all of us and if you track your energy you will see that you have patterns of peaks and troughs of energy in a day. Some may be influenced by sleep, rest and diet which you can influence; others are related to our natural biorhythms. If you are an `early bird' or `lark' you will be full of energy in the mornings. This could be slightly annoying to the `owls' among us who prefer a slower start to the day and reach peak performance by the end of the day.

- You can plan your difficult most challenging work when your energy is high and the easier tasks when you are lower in energy. Also planning breaks when you need to rest is a kindly approach to managing your body – don't force it or push too hard so that you end up in a stress zone. Listen to your body and tune into your feelings. Sometimes we interpret tiredness as unhappiness. It is not the same just simply a signal to rest! For those who look for comfort in alternatives at these times like comfort eating or unhealthy props these are choice moments if you are self-aware. Recognizing your emotional and physical needs to rest or take time out can provide healthier options.

- Regular meals (fuel) and regular breaks (rest) and exercise (energy release) increase our physical well-being. Paying attention to our physical health really does influence our productivity and sense of well-being!

REALITY CHECK – WHERE DOES MY TIME GO?

Time log – keeping a time log can reflect a great deal about how you organize yourself and others. It gives you evidence of your behaviour and your emotional tugs to adopt styles which are either helpful or unhelpful to you. Honestly you may find it quite laborious at first but if you can stand keeping a log for a week you may get some great insights into your patterns of interacting with yourself and others. It involves recording every hour the pattern of activities; the what, who and when of all your interactions. You could use a log like this one:

Time	What	Who

TIME WASTERS?

What are my time wasters?

From your time log you will, among other things, be able to identify time wasters. Some typical time wasters include:

- ▶ Spontaneous distractions
- ▶ Finding/losing things
- ▶ Talking to others (if not intended and no time for)
- ▶ Too much time in meetings
- ▶ Over analysis (paralysis)
- ▶ Postponing unpleasant tasks
- ▶ Starting and never finishing
- ▶ Emails
- ▶ Doing things which aren't central to where your focus is
- ▶ Solving problems which could have been anticipated
- ▶ Unclear communication/confusion
- ▶ … And some others?

_____

_____

_____

ANALYSIS OF MY FOCUS – NOW AND IN THE FUTURE

- ▶ If you gather this information together and compare it with where you wish to spend your time you can create a big picture of how you see yourself now and how you would like to change your time focus for the future. Complete the pie charts below to practice this:

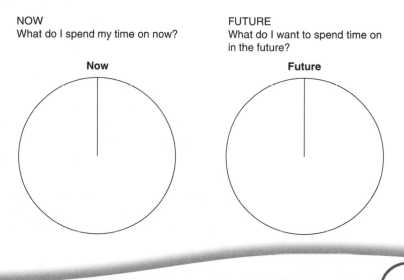

NOW
What do I spend my time on now?

FUTURE
What do I want to spend time on in the future?

Now

Future

TAKE ACTION – WHAT CAN I MOVE FROM REACTIVE TO SCHEDULED?

The next stage is about taking practical action to put your plans in place and inform others of your plans. This may take some careful negotiating as the re allocation of your time and energy is likely to affect others. Generally it may help you use your time more efficiently if you move some of your allocated time from reactive to more scheduled:

 ▷ **Establish boundaries – self-discipline**
 ▷ **Process**
 ▷ **Honour commitment**
 ▷ **Plan for fun/ play time too!**
 ▷ **Manage my diary**
 ▷ **Educate others/help them understand**
 ▷ **Get support from others**
 ▷ **Keep communicating/negotiating my priorities and time/ manage expectations**
 ▷ **Reviews and checkpoints – how am I doing with my/others goals and are we aligned? Do we need to renegotiate?**

DAILY TASKS AND PRESSURES

 ▶ How can I manage daily tasks and pressure?
 ▶ Here are some ideas for thinking about how you organize daily life:

   ▷ **Expectations** – Sometimes we can be overambitious with what we can expect to achieve in a day and end the day with a long list of outstanding tasks to do – very disappointing and demotivating! Being realistic about expectations could be more rewarding and and increase the feel good factor.

   ▷ **The Pareto Principle** also known as the '80/20 Rule' was developed by Joseph M. Juran in 1937. The idea behind the Pareto Principle is that for most us, for most of the time, around 80% of what we achieve comes from just 20% of what we do. In other words, there is a huge imbalance between effort and results. One way of translating this into action is to focus on your top three urgent and important tasks each day – anything else will be a bonus!

   ▷ **Priority setting** – Logging in the urgent and important helps keep a perspective of how you spend your time and helps set priorities (see the model on 'Priority setting') page 152.

▷ **Clear the clutter** – this may take the form of tidying your home, your desk, your personal space or belongings. Having clean clear spaces helps create and promote clear thinking.

▷ **System of working** – overviews, reminders, deadlines, technology; let it work for you and let others know about your systems

▷ **Compartmentalize** – blocking off time for specific activities and having a separate plan for each of them helps you focus on one activity at a time and can help you avoid feeling overwhelmed. Use your mind map to identify those things you wish to address.

▷ **Reward time** – planning to play may sound strange but even as adults we need to play and have fun! Scheduling in play/ relaxation time and planning for work/life balance keeps us vibrant and refreshed.

▷ **Signs/signals of availability** – Letting others know when and how you are available helps you organize your time and helps others feel secure in your relationship with them. If you promise to be available try to follow through – there is nothing more irritating than making arrangements and then being let down, as it not only signals a lack of respect for the other person's time but erodes trust and sends out the wrong message about how you value the other person.

▷ **Manage** interruptions and distractions! Some we have already covered but you may need to assert your needs with compassion. There is more about assertiveness in Chapter 10. Be aware of the self-imposed distractions too, e.g. the butterfly mentality and avoidance tactics, particularly when working on difficult tasks.

▷ **Learn to delegate!** This doesn't just apply to work as you may find delegation useful at home too. The principles of delegation are to hand over responsibility, authority and control so that while you may be accountable, say for paying the mortgage, others know what their areas of responsibility in your house are. Particularly useful when living together and developing a sense of responsibility in our young. At work we can be a little more formal and structured about it, at home and particularly as parents we need to exercise diplomacy and future thinking reward systems to motivate cooperation. Resist temptations to meddle, control and rescue – we all need to be shown how but also need to experience how to overcome difficulty ourselves and build resilience from the learning phases of life!

→ Priority setting

Setting priorities in the best possible way is not an easy task. Many factors are involved, e.g. urgency, importance, relationships with other matters, time required to finish the project, 'political' considerations, personal feelings, etc. **BUT** setting priorities is probably the most important skill in time management.

The idea based on **Dr Stephen Covey's model** of **Urgent/Important Matrix** below may help:

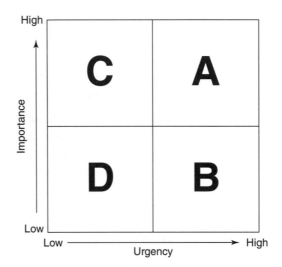

The table shows how different types of tasks, jobs, assignments, meetings, commitments, telephone calls etc. could be handled depending on their relative urgency and importance.

A	*High Urgency/High Importance*	*These should be dealt with as quickly as possible.*
B	*High Urgency/Low Importance*	*These should be dealt with as quickly as possible after A. Maybe delegating to a trusted member of staff will overcome the urgency.*
C	*Low Urgency/High Importance*	*These will probably become urgent soon. Get started on these as soon as time allows. At least do some foundation work.*
D	*Low Urgency/Low Importance*	*Hopefully these can be forgotten. Postponement is a possibility or referral to someone else. Keep an eye on them though.*

➜ My organizing goals?

You may like to set some goals for organizing. Reflect on the following questions:

▶ First steps to success?

▶ Supports?

▶ Potential blocks and ways to overcome them?

_____

_____

_____

_____

_____

_____

_____

_____

_____

_____

_____

_____

_____

_____

_____

_____

YOUR FUTURE VISION AS AN ORGANIZER

So let's now imagine you are a super organizer.

What does that look like?

▶ **Draw a picture of yourself in the bubble below from an organizer's perspective.**

▶ **As an observer, see yourself being and doing the things you know are important to you.**

▶ **Step into the bubble and become what you desire for yourself.**

Away you go!

Summary

- ▶ Our values about time will influence how we manage it.
- ▶ Mindful planning involves raising awareness of past, present and future focus.
- ▶ We have different preferences for planning styles which may support or sabotage us!
- ▶ Taking control of your time and choosing where you want to focus your energy is important for successful organizing of your time!

My learnings from this chapter

_____

_____

_____

_____

_____

_____

Positive thoughts

_____

_____

_____

_____

_____

_____

Where to next

In the next chapter we will look at understanding relationship stress, and how we form and manage win/win relationships.

9 Understanding relationship stress

Poor Amy . . .

Amy was crying on her bed – nothing seemed to be going right in her life! She had split up from her partner and since she had moved in with her mum there had been a great deal of tension between them – she couldn't seem to please her. Her mum had been nagging her about her lack of help around the house and choice of partner too. On top of those pressures she had failed (in her mind) at three interviews for jobs she really wanted – she sobbed at the injustice of her life!

She had met Sam on holiday and they had hit it off straight away. Sam oozed confidence and sureness, something she often felt she lacked. Sam was popular and funny, if a little arrogant, and pursued her relentlessly. It was a whirlwind at the beginning; dates, parties and exciting weekends away. Three years down the line Sam's interest had waned; showing more interest in sport and nights out with friends. Amy felt like she had been abandoned and however much she tried to explain her feelings Sam didn't take her seriously. She had told Sam she wished to end their relationship last week. Sam's response had been to shower her with flattery, flowers and emails. Amy's confusion at this turnaround and promises was making her life even more difficult – what should she do?

We can imagine the inner turmoil Amy may feel about making choices about relationships. We want to feel stimulated, accepted and loved by others but there is always a risk attached to forming relationships – what if we lose them or we are let down by them ? What if it turns out that we're not so loveable and likeable after all?

→ Overview – expectations in relationships

Relationships are all about expectations. How we form, manage and end relationships can be both rewarding and extremely challenging. We look for love and acceptance but risk alienation and rejection too. We all have others' agendas outside of our own to consider and how do we know that we are choosing relationships which are good for us? We go through periods of negotiating and re-negotiating needs and expectations.

Exercise 67:

My relationship challenges

What are your relationship challenges?

Relationship
Challenges

Relationship dynamics affect all aspects of our lives:

THE DATING GAME

In romantic relationships, online dating agencies are making a fortune in attempting to help individuals with the dilemma of creating opportunities to meet their perfect partners. Individuals' time and availability tends to be more squeezed these days and speed dating and cyber relationships fast-track the forming stage. which may be good or bad depending on individual experiences.

Attitudes are changing; some are deeply monogamous others more liberal – there may be many different solutions for aspiring to find the 'perfect match'. Others prefer a more chance and luck approach to meeting Mr or Ms Right. There is so much advice about the formula for a great relationship we get confused about our choices. The idea that there is a perfect match to me seems impossible too.

FAMILY RELATIONSHIPS

In families there are more nuclear (parents and children) and fewer extended family communities, especially around major towns and cities. This can create a 'hole' in the support system and more reliance on each other for support through challenges. Childcare and community support has become more important to us, yet we are much more likely to migrate and even emigrate! Demands for our children to perform well and do well are fuelled by the availability of multiple clubs and activities – fantastic if managed in a balanced way. The 'Flying the nest' process is not necessarily final as parents support their children into adulthood while they get finances in place to move out.

FRIENDSHIPS

In friendships time is less available for socializing especially if you have other commitments. We are more likely to have close circles of good friends and acquaintances and less time for our neighbours unless some kind of special bond develops or there are boundary issues. This is not necessarily bad at all but just different to how many people managed their lives in the past. Working long hours may result in work and social lives merging.

AT WORK

At work relationships seem to be more transactional, measured by performance and results. However, we are seeing a shift and attempts to address the deficit in appreciating human worth and techniques for engagement and excitement at work. I'm working in some amazing cultures which have high concern for employee health and well-being and commitment to developing a sense of vocation, meaning and purpose and appreciation of some old-fashioned values, strengths and virtues. We are, according to the experts, in a post-recession growth period – human capital always has more value in the upturn! This isn't universal though and change is continuous.

→ Your relationship network

Coming back to **YOUR** world we all have networks of relationships which are unique to us.

A framework for this network might look like the following;

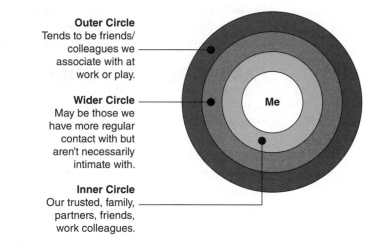

Outer Circle
Tends to be friends/ colleagues we associate with at work or play.

Wider Circle
May be those we have more regular contact with but aren't necessarily intimate with.

Inner Circle
Our trusted, family, partners, friends, work colleagues.

Me

Exercise 68:

My relationship network map

What does your relationship network map – including intimate relationships, close relationships and acquaintances look like?

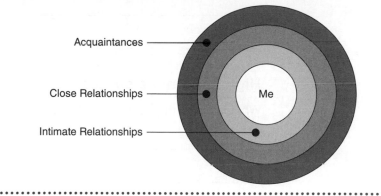

Acquaintances

Close Relationships

Intimate Relationships

Me

FREQUENCY, INTIMACY AND IMPORTANCE?

Record on your relationship map how frequent, intimate and important your relationships are to you:

▶ How important are these relationships to you? (0–10)
▶ How intimate is your relationship with them? (0–10)
▶ How frequent is your contact with them? (0–10)

STRESS AND HAPPINESS?

On the same network map give each person a score according to:

▶ How much STRESS and HAPPINESS do you feel in relation to them?
▶ Indicate ME [S0–S10] and ME [H0–H10]
▶ Putting yourself in their shoes, how much STRESS and HAPPINESS do you imagine they may feel towards you?

Indicate THEY [S0–S10] and THEY [H0–H10]

High stress scores

Describe the issues and causal factors.

_____

_____

_____

_____

_____

_____

High happiness scores

What is it that makes each of these relationships work so well?

_____

_____

_____

_____

_____

_____

When you look at your map are there any things you would change in respect of the following:

Would you add/change any of your relationships?

What could work better?

_____

_____

_____

_____

_____

_____

→ Why do we need relationships?

We have discussed Maslow and the apparent human need for social belonging. John Bowlby's work is also relevant in this respect. Bowlby developed a theory regarding attachment and how the connections we make in early childhood development form a mental and emotional template for our relationships as we develop into adulthood. We need significant carers in infancy to nurture, protect and teach us survival skills.

Sometimes we carry the nature of our childhood caring experiences into adulthood.

→ Relationship attachment styles

Our templates for relationships can be derived from these four styles of intimacy and relating to others:

The Secure style	This is reinforced by stable early childcare.
The Fearful style	Typically early care-giving was inconsistent or overly protective; likely to experience jealousy and disclose information about themselves. They may be clingy and insecure in relationships.
The Dismissive or Avoidant style	A defensive, in-denial and over-positive sense of self stemming from where caregivers were stretched too thin. They are much less likely to experience jealousy and less likely to disclose information about themselves. They are more likely to keep others at a distance.
The Fearful/ Avoidant style	Where the individual may be both anxious and dismissive.

These styles can explain why some prefer a more distant/cool relationship and others a deeper emotional intimacy and there is probably a continuum between the two. I think we all experience times when we need 'space' and autonomy in a relationship and it is an important ingredient for authentic relationships (still maintaining individual identity and perusing individual as well as joint goals). There are also times when we feel more vulnerable and insecure and look for support from others.

Exercise 69:

My relationship attachment style.

What's your prevalent style?	Significant other's prevalent style?
Examples?	*Examples?*

➔ The need for intimacy?

How we form attachments to romantic partners and even friends influences our experience of …

▶ Commitment

▶ Social dominance

▶ Control

▶ Responsibility

- ▶ Intimacy
- ▶ Jealousy
- ▶ Closeness
- ▶ Self-disclosure
- ▶ Conflict
- ▶ Forgiveness
- ▶ Love
- ▶ Lying
- ▶ Infidelity
- ▶ Sexual behaviour
- ▶ … and many more behaviours

Sometimes we automatically play out these roles because of old scripts which no longer serve us and they become relationship irritants, both for us and others. Sometimes they are great strengths. Being self-aware will help you step back and make choices about how you behave and respond to others. As long as they are authentic and really belong to you, stepping into strengths and virtues with courage and compassion which serve you and others will give you a positive vision for moving away from negative states.

Being your **best** self (without trying to be too perfect) will support you!

Exercise 70:

Poor Amy

Amy was looking for love, commitment and intimacy from her partner who seemed happy with a more distant but convenient relationship. Neither was right or wrong, but more importantly it was not meeting Amy's needs.

- ▶ **What do you think Amy's inner critics were saying?**
- ▶ **What were her inner supporters saying?**

Write your thoughts in the table below.

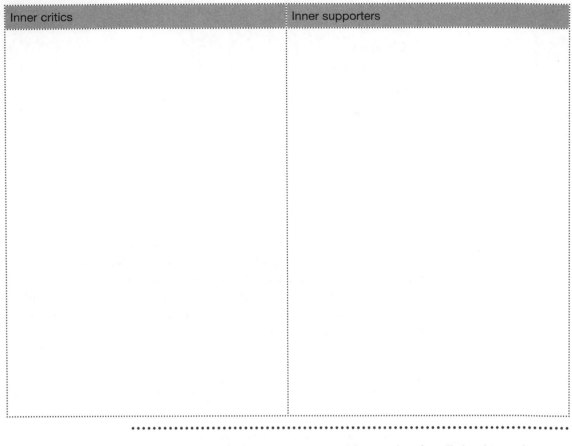

Inner critics	Inner supporters

My guess is the inner critics were blaming her for all the things that weren't right in the relationship and the supporters were congratulating her for having the courage to make a stand!

→ Power in relationships

We all have agendas. The power in relationships can shift and change with different people and different phases in the relationship. It may be the means by which others can utilize their power to influence, control or even manipulate to get what they want. With the right balance between **self-interest** and **altruism** we can negotiate our way through most situations, but it pays to be aware of the different sources of power available to you and those around you and which you can use or abuse!

If too much energy is spent trying to change the other person when they really don't want to change, we can end up feeling disappointed in them and it can be a recipe for conflict, even abuse. Supporting and nurturing others in their interests is very different to trying to force them to change.

Just reflect on that for a moment:

Exercise 71:

Power to change me and others?

▶ Have you experienced others trying to force you to change before?

▶ What was it like on the receiving end?

▶ Have you ever tried to make someone change before?

▶ What was that experience like for you? The other person?

What did you conclude for yourself about these experiences?

_____

_____

_____

_____

_____

_____

_____

_____

_____

→ # Judgementalism and boundaries in relationships

We may try to be non-judgemental and accepting of others but we are unlikely to become completely non-judgemental in relationships because we bring our own perceptions, beliefs, thoughts and memories with us. However being mindful of these things can help us think before we act and speak and consider what belongs to us and to others. It is important to respect the **boundaries** and be aware of when we are crossing over from our **territory** into other people's. This can make others extremely angry and disempower them. It can create a rebellion too!

This doesn't mean that we should stay fixed within our territories but be sensitive to them and find out where sensitivities lie in order to empathize and negotiate with others.

An example of this is:

Amy's mother

By passing judgement on Amy's choice of partner Amy's mother was crossing into dangerous territory. When Amy was younger she may have had an influence on her choice of relationship. However, she risked alienating Amy by interfering with the way she managed her relationship, and through her lack of trust in Amy's ability to handle the situation and make her own mind up. By attempting to rescue her she also risked denying Amy the opportunity to learn from her mistakes and to build her self-confidence in her ability to make the right choices. There is a delicate line between being asked and invited for an opinion, supporting others and trying to control and manipulate freedom of choice.

These dynamics can appear in friendships and at work too!

FORGIVENESS

Amy discussed these issues with her mum and both described how they felt. They forgave each other for the hurt they may have unintentionally caused. After all they loved and valued each other!

THE SPOILED CHILD SYNDROME

While on the subject of parenting, in 1989 **Bruce McIntosh** coined the term the '**Spoiled Child Syndrome**'.

It involved:

▶ Failure of parents to enforce consistent, age-appropriate limits.

▶ Parents shielding the child from normal everyday frustrations.

▶ Provision of excessive material gifts, even when the child has not behaved properly.

- ▶ Improper role models provided by parents.
- ▶ Tantrums and demanding behaviour translate to adulthood together with a sense of 'entitlement'!

Growing up with a sense of entitlement is not a good experience for anyone in any relationship and potentially creates lose/lose outcomes. Whether you are the parent or the grown-up child to get to win/win involves harnessing courage to change, reframing these beliefs and taking a fresh look at self-responsibility.

→ Self-responsibility and problem ownership

Self-responsibility is a secret to success in relationships. Why a secret? Because it is often avoided or discounted possibly because of pride and it involves courage, effort and honesty with ourselves.

We can expend enormous amounts of energy finding solutions outside of ourselves to the point of denial, anything to avoid changing what we know and is comfortable. This is often wasted energy! What is really needed is to sit down with ourselves as if our best friend and give ourselves a good talking to and accept what we need to take responsibility for in order to move forward. Blame, denial, resistance and excuses are our internal enemies when it comes to taking responsibility and if you can challenge and overcome these internal voices, you will have unlocked a secret power within you to make things happen and for others to trust you more!

Exercise 72:

My territory and others' territory

Take a good honest look through win/win glasses and evaluate what you think is reasonably your territory and others' territory:

My territory	Others' territory
I have ownership/responsibility for:	Others have ownership/responsibility for:

Depending on your beliefs you will have different ideas about what you/ others are responsible for.

We of course have to agree on and negotiate with other people if we are going to work together.

→ Forming romantic relationships

Exercise 73:

Forming relationships and managing endings

▶ Do you remember forming an important romantic relationship? What was it like for you?

_____

_____

_____

_____

▶ Have you ever had to end a relationship? What was it like for you?

_____

_____

_____

_____

▶ How did you manage the ending?

_____

_____

_____

_____

Managing endings is never easy but if you can do so with respect, courage and compassion, allowing for the inevitable grief which surrounds the loss, then you and whoever is involved will have a fighting chance of coming to terms with the ending over time. In romantic relationships ending one relationship before starting another is always cleaner and models integrity. Taking betrayal out of the equation also helps others cope with the potential feelings of rejection. If you are experiencing distress over the ending of a relationship it is important to get support from close family, friends, counselling or other sources of talking therapy.

THE LIST!

After I experienced my second divorce I vowed to spend time to experience life on my own and to discover what I valued in relationships before entering another one. I developed a rich and full life for myself but when I felt the time was right to have another relationship I created 'THE LIST.'

I decided that if I was going to have another relationship it had to add value to my and the 'mystery person's' life.

This was a list of what I did want in a relationship and what I didn't want. It included:

Qualities /Strengths?	Values?	Life position? (e.g. age/job/life/stage)
Intelligent (IQ and EQ)	Family /community/friends	Unattached from ex partners
Interested in people/sociable	Loyalty	Financially independent and solvent
Curious about life	Interest in exploring/adventures	Freedom for new experiences
Caring/respectful	Enjoys intimacy	Ambitious to live life to the full
Supportive	Fair	Ambitious to build a rich full life together
Brave	Values fidelity	
Organized	Companionship	
Fun		
Knows his own mind		
A 'can do' mentality		
Physical attraction		

As soon as I had written my list I met my husband! I saw an advert the following day in a local paper, posted by an old fashioned local 'match maker'. When we met we felt instantly drawn to each other … the rest is history! Some may call it luck but I call it synchronicity. Of course I didn't show him the list. Over time we discovered our values matched and I met his requirements too.

My list may not be the same as yours. You'll notice that 'interest in operas' and 'tall dark and handsome' didn't figure anywhere on my list. For me it was mainly about shared values and attitudes towards life. I can understand how arranged marriages work in this respect – our networks of like-minded friends and family are potentially valuable links to others. Of course there is chemistry too which is very individual and in my view very necessary. I know some are attracted to opposites which present different challenges but it doesn't mean to say that the relationships can't work with skilled negotiation and flexible mindedness!

There was a message here for me in preparing my list:

▶ It makes sense to be you at the beginning of relationships;

▶ It makes sense to know you before choosing a relationship!

Exercise 74:

My list

If you think about the forming of an important relationship what **was** or **is** on your list?

Qualities /Strengths?	Values?	Life position?

STAGES OF FORMING ROMANTIC RELATIONSHIPS

Dr Susan Campbell (author of *Saying What's Real*, 2005) conducted a study of hundreds of couples as they went through the stages of forming romantic relationships:

The Romance Stage	The 'in love' intoxicating stage
The Power Struggle Stage	Trying to change your partner – why aren't you like when we first met? Why can't you be more like me?
The Stability Stage	If you've completed the Power Struggle stage, a more mature form than in the Romance stage develops.
The Commitment Stage	You accept that you and your partner are human and that your relationship has shortcomings and you choose each other consciously.
The Co-Creation or Bliss Stage	In this stage you become two people who have chosen to be a team moving out into the world. Often, couples in this stage work on a project together – some kind of shared creative work that is intended to contribute to the world in some way, e.g. a business, a charity or a family.

Exercise 75:

Stage of my relationship?

If you are in a relationship – what stage might you be in? Use the table below to write notes and identify what stage you are at in your relationship.

The Romance Stage	The Power Struggle Stage	The Stability Stage	The Commitment Stage	The Co-Creation or Bliss Stage

→ Win/win and building relationships

What we want to do regardless of our histories is create stability in relationships and enjoy time with our relationships. We can do this in many ways – here are a few ideas:

- ▶ Recognizing others' individuality and separateness
- ▶ Only giving feedback which is fundamentally in their best interests
- ▶ Expressing love and admiration for their qualities
- ▶ Offering support and praise for their achievements
- ▶ Reinforcing the value of them as an authentic important person

Of course at the same time we want to endeavour to collaborate and respect others' differences, as we live in co-dependent communities after all.

In working environments we may not be able to realistically achieve the above and 'respecting others' may be more important than having to like everyone we work with.

➔ Using courage and compassion to invest in your relationships

No relationship is going to be conflict free; we all have out 'Hot Buttons'! Learning to disagree, negotiate and agree on expectations is a continuing loop.

Review   Discuss

Sometimes it takes courage to confront sensitive issues, particularly if they are trespassing on your territory. But if we do so with compassion and 'humanness' we generally all appreciate it when someone cares enough about us to listen.

➔ Managing relationships positively

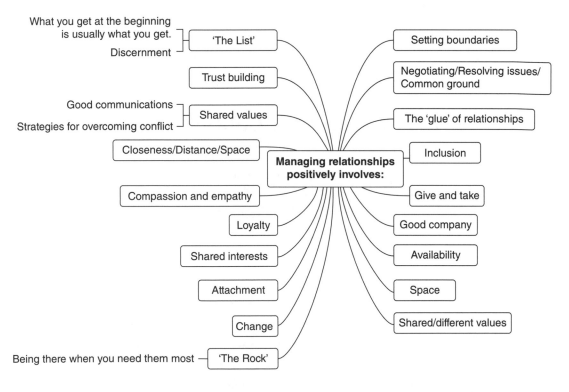

What you get at the beginning is usually what you get.
Discernment — 'The List'

Trust building

Good communications
Strategies for overcoming conflict — Shared values

Closeness/Distance/Space

Compassion and empathy

Loyalty

Shared interests

Attachment

Change

Being there when you need them most — 'The Rock'

Managing relationships positively involves:

Setting boundaries

Negotiating/Resolving issues/Common ground

The 'glue' of relationships

Inclusion

Give and take

Good company

Availability

Space

Shared/different values

→ And finally ...

I maintain that successful relationships involve:

▶ Gradual learning about each other to understand each other's values

▶ Making choices which match each other's needs and agree on expectations

▶ Clear and continuous communication about each other's changing needs

Summary

▶ Relationships are about expectations.

▶ We may have different needs for attachment and intimacy.

▶ Our inner critics and inner supporters can keep us safe or sabotage us.

▶ Understanding your own and others' territories helps lead to compromise.

▶ Taking ownership of your thoughts, actions and emotions and respecting others to do the same makes you more powerful and trustworthy.

▶ Discernment in choosing relationships can pay off.

▶ Win/win involves courage, compassion and forgiveness.

▶ Maintaining healthy relationships involves continuous communication and flexible negotiating!

My learnings from this chapter

_____

_____

_____

_____

_____

_____

Positive thoughts

_____

_____

_____

_____

_____

_____

Where to next?

In the next chapter we will look at how to communicate assertively with courage and compassion.

10 Communicating with courage and compassion

Dave's dilemma

Dave liked harmony. If he could avoid conflict he would and up to now as a specialist in his scientific field he had managed to keep his head down and navigate the politics of his organization. He now faced a dilemma. He was being encouraged to take a promotion which would involve managing a team and representing the department at meetings.

He partly relished the idea and felt flattered that his potential was being recognized but another part of him was filled with dread at the thought of managing relationships, performance and inter-departmental conflicts. When he thought about it this had been a pattern throughout his life and at home he tended to avoid situations involving conflict.

This had been a contributing factor to disagreements with his wife as he found setting the boundaries with his kids really difficult resulting in him being too soft or flipping to too tough a stance under pressure.

→ Communicating with courage and compassion

When I think about my favourite role models as communicators a few stand out. One includes Mandela. Another deep in my memory is a boss who I witnessed a few times speaking at the Council of Europe. I watched in awe at his elegance of delivery, confidence and conviction in conveying his message and how everyone stopped and listened when he spoke. Even the translators up in the 'gods' seemed struck by his presence. He had a charisma which immediately earned respect; he knew his topic and was passionate about what he had to say. He proposed far reaching ideas for the good of member states. Perhaps he was an example of someone stepping into his strengths and virtues with ease.

I am often filled with the same awe when listening to some of the wonderful professors I work with at London Business School. Their warmth, humour and engagement is something to behold in the pursuit of helping others grasp sometimes difficult and complex ideas and transforming them into easily accessible lessons.

When thinking about my most powerful story tellers and influencers, I realize that they are those who do so with courage and compassion. The story line is about overcoming adversity and bringing people and communities together with courage and compassion.

 *Exercise 76:*

Your favourite communicators

▶ Who are your favourite communicators?

_____

_____

_____

_____

_____

► What do you admire about them?

_____

_____

_____

_____

_____

 We all have a story and don't have be world famous or public speakers to demonstrate courage and compassion but can influence small everyday challenges which make a difference. Overcoming adversity in actions and deeds, using our wisdom rather than impulse is a great skill which we can all master if mindful and consequently make better decisions and choices about our own and others' lives.

→ Dave's dilemma

Dave's dilemma was about him grappling with his own courage to make a decision about his future and not feeling confident about his abilities to take on additional responsibilities. He tended to avoid conflict and assumed the new role would only involve conflict; that giving his kids boundaries and limits would involve too much conflict; gross overgeneralizations when you think about the other opportunities he may create for himself and others. We all face decisions like this, 'shall we, shan't we?' especially if it's going to involve interactions with others of our species!

Sometimes we avoid conflict because:

► We fear what others will think of us;
► We imagine the worst consequences;
► We prefer our comfortable but unchanging worlds.

The intolerance of negative feelings, and the belief that we must feel 100 per cent positive or comfortable at all times, can limit our ability to do what is good and right.

The black dustbin liner

Jack had had enough of not being able to walk into his son Ben's room without tripping over toys stacked high. He had tried asking nicely, nagging and even threats but none had worked and the pile was steadily getting higher. He felt angry, disrespected and frustrated with himself too for not being able to get Ben to tidy up. He shared the problem with his friend over a drink after work one night. His friend asked him:

'What are the consequences of Ben not tidying up?' and 'What do you want Ben to learn?'

Jack then realized that he passionately wanted Ben to learn to take responsibility for his mess, to learn and engage with it rather than be nagged into it. He felt it was an important metaphor for life and he wanted Ben growing up to be kind, respectful and considerate for the sake of all his future relationships. He then had a brainwave. He asked Ben again to tidy up and gave him three warnings. If on the third warning he didn't tidy up, Jack would be placing all his toys in black dustbin liners and Ben would then have to sort through to find them. He also suggested that if he had toys he didn't want, he could arrange to take him to a 'Boot Fair' and make some pocket money for him.

Of course there was no change, so Jack steeled himself and followed his plan through. When Ben walked into his bedroom after school he shouted and stamped his feet at the injustice. After an hour he calmed down and Jack crept up to the bedroom where he observed Ben through the crack in the door quietly and systematically placing his toys carefully and tidily around his bedroom. Jack congratulated him and they had fun together at the 'Boot Fair'. Jack also noticed how Ben always tidied up after himself from then on and there was a shift in his relationship; Ben was more respectful and the sense of entitlement had disappeared. Jack had acted with courage and compassion for the long-term benefit of his son.

→ Assertiveness with courage and compassion

This chapter is about developing the skills to help us communicate. When we have skills we develop confidence to do rather than avoid (unless there is good reason to do so). Avoidance (or being too nice) and aggression can create stress in our lives unnecessarily.

→ What's your script?

We have already discussed that at work or play we can repeat the scripts learned from the past even though they may no longer be relevant or helpful to us and this can affect how we relate to others. We learn from early reinforcements and criticisms how to adapt in different situations and these become our scripts; subconsciously reminded by our inner voice or self-talk. The inner/outer critics can make enormous demands upon us and also on others!

My script?

Here are some examples of self-talk relating to relationships. Tick those relevant to you and add any additional examples you can think of:

- ▶ I must respect my elders ☐
- ▶ I must please others ☐
- ▶ Everyone must like me ☐
- ▶ I must get it right ☐
- ▶ I mustn't show my sad or angry feelings ☐
- ▶ I must meet others' needs ☐
- ▶ I must be strong ☐
- ▶ I must be responsible ☐
- ▶ I must be capable ☐
- ▶ I must win, come what may! ☐
- ▶ I must make a good impression ☐
- ▶ I must associate with the right people ☐
- ▶ I must visit my mother twice a week ☐

- ▶ I must get what I want ☐
- ▶ I must be successful ☐
- ▶ I must be accepted ☐
- ▶ I must be perfect ☐
- ▶ I must be loved! ☐

Do you have any others?

_____

_____

_____

_____

Some of these are appropriate to certain situations and some are grossly inappropriate.

The reframing model TAPES can be helpful in developing some healthy thinking patterns and responses to the less desirable elements of these demands.

➜ The assertiveness model

Sometimes others have differing self-driven agendas and their own insecurities and we can allow others to undermine us by:

Aggression	Indirect Aggression
- being aggressive or intimidating us	- manipulating us
- insulting us or criticizing the way we look/what we do	- whinging and whining
- bragging and competing with us	- withdrawing co-operation
- judging us negatively	- hiding information which could benefit us
- trying to change us	- veiled criticism
- threats	- emotional blackmail
- forcing their need on us for their own gain	- sulking
- convincing us of their sense of entitlement	- poor me
- trying to convince us we are wrong and they are right!	- victim /martyr

	- sarcasm
	- try to live vicariously through us
	- marginalizing us
	- ignoring us
	- leaving us out

Equally we can try to do the same to others. These behaviours are not recommended as they again are relationship irritants and undermine trust.

ASSERTIVENESS – A WIN/WIN MODEL

Alternatively we can choose to communicate assertively with courage and compassion which includes:

▶ Clear and direct communication

▶ Expressing your needs and respecting others' needs

▶ Understanding and empathizing with others

▶ Communicating with honesty and integrity

▶ In other words win/win!

Does that sound boring?

Well it doesn't need to be – you still have your personality after all with all your talents, strengths and virtues – we are all different and can celebrate those differences!

If we put this into a model of assertiveness it looks like this:

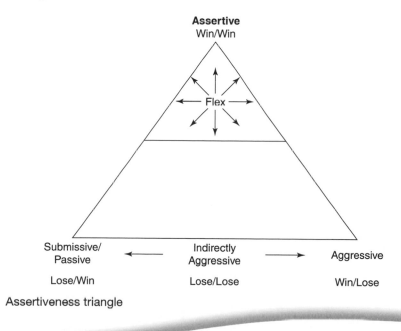

Assertiveness triangle

Place an 'X' where you feel you are in the Assertiveness Triangle above. This is a reflection of your most naturally felt style. If you are honest about where you feel you are, you can move from this place when you feel it is appropriate.

I recommend that you don't aim to operate in the extremes of Submissive/Passive or Aggressive, but flex within the top half of the triangle.

AGGRESSION IN COMMUNICATION – WIN/LOSE

This is a directly competitive stance and to be used with care! It is questionable in relationships although from a business perspective you could argue that companies are competitive when fighting for the same business – but is aggression necessary?

In sport we see channelled aggression but competitors tend to be competing with themselves and often shake hands afterwards.

Dominance and disrespect tends to lead to breakdowns in relationships starting with verbal and at worst progressing to physical.

The aggression cycle

Health warning!

Both aggressive, indirectly aggressive and passive styles can create serious health issues and impact well-being!

INDIRECT AGGRESSION – LOSE/LOSE

These are behaviours like talking behind others' backs, sulking, and indirect non-cooperation. This gets you noticed (think teenagers) but not in a good way and tends to make others frustrated and angry. It also models distrust.

PASSIVITY – LOSE/WIN

What we have established so far is that being 'too nice' or 'passive' also has its consequences:

Take the example of not saying no!

→ Excessive niceness example: Saying no (or not!)

Let's consider failing to say no to a request that you are not happy about taking on. Say a friend asks you to babysit. You may be very happy to do so but if you are not and say yes to please your friend, you potentially invite stress in yourself and potentially damage the trust and openness in the relationship. This could also impact how you choose to use your time and distract you from your own focus. You can kick yourself for not being honest in the first place and possibly secretly blame and avoid your friend so that you don't have to deal with a similar issue again! Then comes the guilt and shame at not having handled the situation well in the first place!

Exercise 78:

Saying 'no'

▶ Can you remember a situation where you failed to say no and regretted it?

_____

_____

_____

_____

_____

▶ What was your reason for saying yes?

_____

_____

_____

_____

_____

▶ What were the consequences?

- for you

_____

_____

_____

- for other(s)

_____

_____

_____

The webs we weave to avoid conflict! If you believe that you must please others at all times and use misplaced guilt as your moral compass, it could affect your self-esteem. One issue can have many consequences to your inner and outer worlds. Acting on impulse often results in regret – we are aiming for **mindful** action and choices so that we think before we act.

Communicating assertively, with courage and compassion can avoid a great deal of stress and helps build relationships.

→ Privileges

It helps with assertiveness if we have a moral compass about what we can expect from ourselves and others.

Here is a questionnaire based on the work of one of the valued influencers in my life **Nancy Paul** (author of *The Right to be YOU*). It was originally designed at a time when **'rights'** and **'asserting rights'** was considered the most important influencing tactic. However, too much expression of rights in relationships now can be negatively interpreted as a **'sense of entitlement'** which people generally react badly to.

I have replaced the word rights with the word privilege for this reason. I believe also that if we exercise the privileges with courage and compassion, we can be more effective.

Exercise 79:

My privileges?

Indicate below whether you agree or disagree with each idea and add your own ideas to the list:

MY PRIVILEGES:

			Disagree	Agree
1.	PRIVILEGE	Set and hold my own values and priorities.		
	RESPONSIBILITY	As long as it does me no harm or you no harm.		

2.	PRIVILEGE	To be treated with respect.		
	RESPONSIBILITY	To treat others with respect.		
3.	PRIVILEGE	To be listened to and taken seriously.		
	RESPONSIBILITY	To talk in a clear way and listen to others.		
4.	PRIVILEGE	To express my own feelings and beliefs.		
	RESPONSIBILITY	To be responsible for the consequences.		
5.	PRIVILEGE	Ask for what I want.		
	RESPONSIBILITY	To allow others to do so.		
6.	PRIVILEGE	To say 'no' without paying for it with guilt or other deeds.		
	RESPONSIBILITY	To say 'yes' when I mean 'yes' and 'no' when I mean 'no'.		

7.	PRIVILEGE	To get all information relevant to me?		
	RESPONSIBILITY	To ask for that information.		
8.	PRIVILEGE	Make mistakes which are part of the learning process.		
	RESPONSIBILITY	To learn from my mistakes.		
9.	PRIVILEGE	To be the judge of my own worth, time and expertise.		
	RESPONSIBILITY	To use information I have received from people I value.		
10.	PRIVILEGE	Choose to act passively or assertively as the situation requires it.		
	RESPONSIBILITY	To be responsible for the consequences.		
11.	OTHER PRIVILEGES AND RESPONSIBILITIES?			

You will notice that all these **Privileges** and **Responsibilities** involve being assertive and making/thinking choices rather than just mindlessly reacting!

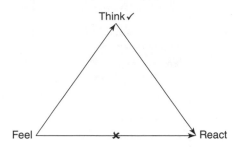

There will also be many more that are invisible to ourselves and others, so finding out and not assuming we know what others feel or want is important. This is where listening and questioning skills come in!

→ Listening and questioning skills

Here is a quick and easy model for listening dos and don'ts:

Listening and responding		Questions	
Do	Don't	Do	Don't
✓ Be present	✗ Interrupt	✓ Open questions	✗ Leading questions
✓ Give space for responding	✗ Jump to conclusions	- Tell me more?	- (leads others to your assumptions)
✓ Summarize	✗ Think about something else/ your experiences	- How?/What?	✗ Closed questions (lead to Yes/No answers).
✓ Reflect – on meaning/feelings		- Where?/When?	
✓ Show empathy and interest		✓ Specific questions	
		✓ Checking questions	

Exercise 80:

Listening practice

Think about something which you would like to discuss with someone. It could be a small, but important issue. Set yourself the goal of listening to them properly.

Prepare yourself below for this event:

Issue?	Who with?	Your goal for listening?	Time/place?	The mindful skills you will use?

→ Getting to win/win

Be aware that listening is not the same as manipulating and it may be that your goal is simply to understand the other person's point of view. Hopefully by modelling listening skills, you will encourage the other person to do the same. Having 'a voice' leads to 'understanding'; you can then agree a new way forward to meet both your needs!

If you are in a professional negotiating role, you may use this investigative style in the understanding of others' needs.

Having a voice → Understanding → Agreeing a way forward →

→ What is your style as a communicator?

Even if you practise compassion mindfully and with the best of intentions, when you are under pressure, it is easy to come across as tense, harsh or formal. This will be picked up by the recipient first and foremost, regardless of the message.

As part of our instinctive **'Friend or Foe'** appraisals, we are very good at reading people and according to **Professor Albert Mehrabian's** studies of body language in the 1960s, we interpret behaviour we like or dislike according to the messages we pick up from facial expressions, vocal style and words used.

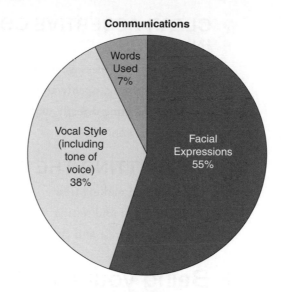

Communications

- Words Used 7%
- Vocal Style (including tone of voice) 38%
- Facial Expressions 55%

What does this mean for the way we communicate?

_____

_____

_____

_____

→ So communicating involves?

Clearly, style matters – prepare for:

▶ Facial expressions

▶ Tone of voice

▶ Volume

▶ Pace

▶ Body language

COURAGEOUS AND COMPASSIONATE COMMUNICATION INVOLVES:

▶ Being brave enough to deal with unresolved issues

▶ Listening, asking questions and understanding others' perspectives

▶ Acting in the long-term interests of both/all

▶ Showing empathy when appropriate

CLEAR ASSERTIVE COMMUNICATION INVOLVES:

▶ Having a clear message about your intentions

▶ Communicating openly and honestly

▶ Communicating directly with the person involved

▶ Getting to win/win

AND SETTING THE ENVIRONMENT:

▶ Timing and making time

▶ Environment and setting

▶ Showing interest and curiosity

→ Being your own best friend

If you follow the principle that we should treat others as we would like to be treated ourselves, it then follows that we should treat ourselves as we would treat others. This is what being your own best friend means. You can choose how you want to be:

▶ **Passive**/accommodating when necessary

▶ **Assertive**/able to express your needs, collaborate and engage

▶ **Aggressive**/fight/stand up for yourself when necessary

Perhaps these are styles you adopt with different people in different situations too?

Exercise 81:

Self-diagnosis – communication issues?

If you think about communication issues what/who are they with? What style do you adopt with them? Why this style?

▶ **Situations?/Communication issues?**

_____

_____

_____

▶ People?

_____

_____

_____

_____

_____

▶ Style I adopt?

_____

_____

_____

_____

▶ What could I do differently?

_____

_____

_____

_____

_____

....

→ Some specific assertiveness skills

Here are some specific assertiveness skills you can use to prepare
yourself for some scenarios.

GETTING WHAT YOU WANT/NEED FROM OTHERS

It is your privilege to make requests; others have the privilege to refuse.

Tips

- Ask politely and clearly
- Don't apologize
- Be direct
- Be brief
- Give a reason if it helps
- Don't oversell
- Don't hint or ask indirectly

REFUSING REQUESTS

It is others' privilege to ask and your privilege to say 'no' without feeling guilty. Listen to your immediate gut reaction – it is the best guide to whether you really want to say 'yes' or 'no'. If you need to, ask for time.

Tips

- Ask for clarification
- Keep your reply brief
- Say 'no' clearly and directly (or an equivalent, such as 'I don't want … '/'I'd prefer not …').
- Give a brief (genuine) reason
- Give evidence of the impact of saying yes if it helps
- Don't apologize profusely
- Offer a compromise if feasible
- Acknowledge requester's feelings – e.g. 'I can see this will cause you difficulties.'

If the person persists or becomes manipulative, try the 'broken record' technique:

- Choose a suitable phrase, using 'I'
- Keep repeating it (but not in a hostile way)
- Don't be distracted – stay firmly with your phrase and resist the temptation to answer or respond to possible insults.

RECEIVING FEEDBACK AND CRITICISM

It is important to learn to receive feedback and criticism in a constructive way, because feedback from others is an important source of information about us and creates understanding.

Non-valid or unfair criticism – the 'So what?' test

If it is non-valid, decide whether it passes the 'So what?' test, i.e. whether or not it matters that the person continues with that opinion.

If it **DOESN'T** matter, use the 'fogging' technique:

Tips

▶ Listen carefully

▶ Don't deny – this provides the critic with more communication

▶ Respond only to what the other person SAYS (not implies)

▶ Use fogging statements such as 'You may be right', 'That is a point', 'I can understand why you would think that', 'Yes, I probably seem rather stubborn about that'.

The FOGGING technique is useful because, while acknowledging that there may be some truth in what the critic says, you remain your own judge over what you do.

If it **DOES** matter:

▶ Reply assertively that you do not agree

▶ Keep calm and neutral but firm

▶ Give a reason for your opinion/disagreement, if relevant

Put-downs

If you think the other person is putting you down it is important to deal with it. Put-downs usually come from indirect aggression:

▶ Reply assertively how it makes you feel

▶ If they do a double put-down e.g. 'You take things too seriously', 'You have no sense of humour', do not let it put you off.

Receiving fair criticism

If the criticism is valid and constructive, accept it without letting it escalate:

Tips

▶ Thank them for the feedback

▶ Listen carefully

▶ Do not counter-criticize

- ▶ Ask for the reasons behind the statement
- ▶ Try to elicit useful, constructive feedback (examples, more information)
- ▶ If necessary, joint problem-solve.

Making a mistake

If you recognize that you have made a mistake:

Tips

- ▶ Admit it openly
- ▶ Say sorry once and mean it
- ▶ Do not counter-attack, also do not over-apologize, e.g. 'I hadn't realized I kept interrupting you – I know it is a really annoying habit – I'll try to be more aware of what I'm doing in the future.'

Accepting compliments

Many of us feel uncomfortable about accepting genuine compliments.

Tips

- ▶ Smile and thank the person.
- ▶ Be brief, e.g. 'Thank you. I'm glad you like it.'

Giving feedback and criticism

Many of us dislike giving positive or negative feedback to others, but it will be helpful to the receiver if you:

Tips

- ▶ Time it properly
- ▶ Get their version of events
- ▶ Listen
- ▶ Concentrate on things which can be modified
- ▶ Use specific examples; be direct, honest and supportive
- ▶ Describe the behaviour rather than judge the person
- ▶ Deal with defence reactions positively
- ▶ Use 'I' statements (not 'you')
- ▶ Use positive reinforcement
- ▶ Review what has been agreed/learned

Dealing with anger from others

The most useful strategy is to distance yourself psychologically and not engage in an unconstructive argument.

Tips

▶ Listen

▶ Clarify

▶ Don't argue back

▶ Recognize that the person is angry, e.g. 'I can see you are very angry about this.'

▶ State your case assertively

▶ Use a calm voice

▶ Problem-solve (together if possible)

Where someone is being quite unreasonable, allow yourself the right to walk away.

Dealing with your own anger

Anger is a natural (and useful) emotion – we all experience it, but not all of us are able to deal with it constructively. An important first step is to recognize your anger and accept responsibility for your angry feelings. Identify the real source.

Tips

▶ Use 'I'. 'I am very angry …' 'It bothers me that …' 'I am upset about …'

▶ Use appropriate body languages, e.g. avoid the inappropriate smile, gritted teeth, etc.

▶ Give a clear message where you want a change of behaviour or attitude from the other person, e.g. 'I would like …' 'I would prefer …' 'Please will you …'

▶ Where you meet resistance, use 'gears'. Take a calm, staged approach as follows:

   i Polite low-level statement, 'I would prefer you not to shout at me.'

   ii Intensify statement by stepping up verbally and non-verbally, 'I insist you stop shouting at me.'

   iii Spell out the consequences. 'If you continue, I shall have to end this conversation!'

   iv Carry out the consequences.

It is vital to give each message in a neutral, factual and confident manner and not deliver them as threats. This indicates an assertive stance and gives the other person the chance to provide a solution without resorting to enforcing consequences.

Depersonalize the issue rather than seeing yourself in the middle of it. See yourself as the observer looking in!

→ Planning for communicating with courage and compassion

My communications goal

Take one example of a communicating issue you would like to resolve with someone.

Use the planning tool below to prepare for the situation:

The person/ context	The issue between us?	My goal/Their possible goal?	What choices do I have/they have?	How will I approach the issue?	How will I know if the outcome is positive for me/them?

Summary

- ▶ Avoidance and aggression in communication can be destructive.
- ▶ Communicating assertively involves courage and compassion.
- ▶ Our 'scripts' can support or sabotage us.
- ▶ Assertiveness is a win/win model.
- ▶ Being aware of yours and others' moral compasses helps you tread carefully and respectfully towards negotiating win/win.
- ▶ With practice the skills can become part of your tool box!

My learnings from this chapter

_____

_____

_____

_____

_____

_____

Positive thoughts

_____

_____

_____

_____

_____

_____

Where to next?

 In the next chapter we will look at how you can improve your overall sense of well-being.

Mindfulness and well-being

In this chapter we will cover:
- ▶ What is health and well-being?
- ▶ The wheel of well-being
- ▶ Mindfulness and cognitive behavioural techniques
- ▶ Managing our thoughts, actions, physical health and emotions

A tale of two extremes …

Laura

Laura realized as she sat staring into space, that she had lost touch with herself. Her life felt isolated and devoid of purpose. She had given up her job, her hobbies and her friends for the sake of comfort. Her self-esteem had hit rock bottom. She had started to put on weight, was drinking a bottle of wine every night, her sleep patterns were shot to pieces and she felt bored, uninspired and depressed …

Eric

Eric had been working himself into the ground for years. He had to admit that he was a workaholic and possibly an alcoholic. He had started off loving his job and gradually as he had directed all his efforts towards being successful he had lost himself to it. Food, drink and smoking were emotional props for him. He had no time for relationships and couldn't see a way out …

These two stories are not untypical and remind me of how our minds can play tricks with us about what is good for us. Laura was in a comfort trap; Eric had pushed himself into a Stress Zone. They were both possibly feeling trapped and experiencing depression.

→ What is well-being?

> *'Health is a state of complete physical, mental and social well-being and not merely the absence of disease or infirmity.'*
>
> World Health Organization

This definition has not been amended since 1948.

THE PRINCIPLE OF OSCILLATION

Jim Loehr, a well-known sports psychologist, says that to be a peak performer in any area, you have to find ways to renew your energy – physically, emotionally, mentally and spiritually. He talks about how our body's energy systems work best when we turn them on – and then turn them off again.

This is the principle of oscillation – intense energy expenditure followed by gentle energy recovery.

A RECIPE FOR BALANCE

In **Chapter 3** we looked at how if we are over-challenged over a long period of time, our performance goes down and can result in depression or breakdown. If under-challenged, we can become bored and disengaged.

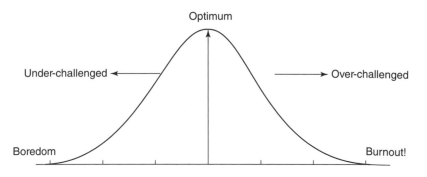

The trick to performing at your optimum and feeling great is finding your balance. Craft your environment and conditions to support **you!**

ENLIGHTENED SELF-INTEREST

We have also explored enlightened self-interest and compassion for yourself throughout this book, so here is a chance to put yourself 'centre stage' to examine and pay attention to what is happening in your world.

THE WHEEL OF WELL-BEING

I have created this wheel of well-being based on some of the principles and recommendations for happiness and well-being discussed already in this book. Creating your own wheel of well-being will also increase your resilience!

I have added in here the 'Spirit' as an important element to us feeling moved and motivated to connecting to a major purpose outside of us.

Exercise 83:

Which zone are you in?

Which zone do you think you are in at present?

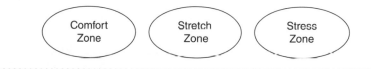

Comfort Zone · Stretch Zone · Stress Zone

→ # Depression

I mentioned in **Chapter 3** that if you think you are depressed it is a good idea to see your doctor to get a proper diagnosis. Low moods tend to improve after a short time but a low mood that doesn't go away can be a sign of depression. If you are feeling depressed you are not alone; millions suffer from depression at different times in their lives and you can do something about it, especially if you use it as an opportunity to learn new strategies for coping and developing your resilience. There are some pointers for how to develop these strategies in this workbook based on the tried and tested methods of cognitive behavioural therapy, mindfulness and stress management. If you are clinically depressed you may need medical intervention, such as antidepressants. There are also other sources of treatment including:

▶ EFT – Emotional Freedom Techniques

▶ Hypnotherapy

▶ Reiki

▶ Acupuncture

▶ Yoga

▶ Reflexology

▶ Meditation

▶ Homeopathy

▶ … and many others!

→ Mood chart

If you want to track your moods you can use the mood chart below together with a thought log.

My mood chart and thought log

Using a daily mood chart may be very revealing. It is not just to identify if you are depressed but also to see what, by association, affects your moods. None of us are completely stable; we all go through ups and downs especially in response to our biorhythms. Some of us are 'owls' and function best later in the day, while some of us are 'larks' and early birds. We may also experience physical dips after a meal as the blood rushes to the digestion system. Lack of exercise and too few breaks between effort, can also cause our systems to temporarily crash.

Remember **Jim Loehr's** 'principle of oscillation' at the beginning of this chapter? He also used the metaphor 'Life is not a marathon – it is a series of sprints.'

Example – Mood chart

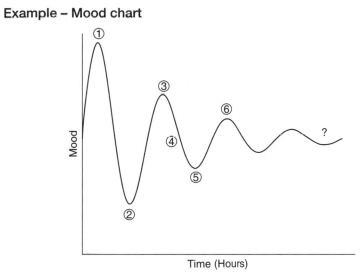

Mood chart

Plot your mood today, or tomorrow if you prefer, and see what emerges. At each peak or trough allocate a consecutive number. It is best to do this in the moment. The idea is to plot your ups and downs and any other variations you choose:

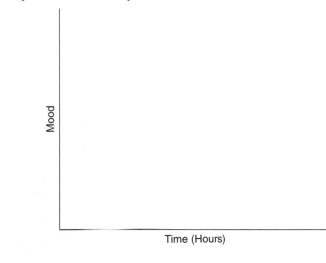

My Mood chart

Thought log

As you plot your course on the mood chart simultaneously log your Thoughts, Actions, Physical Responses and Emotions against each numbered point in time. It is arguable whether thoughts lead emotions or the other way around, what is more important is the patterns this logging reveals to you.

If you can bear it, try logging your moods and thoughts over a week (if it is a typical week). The insights could prove invaluable!

	Thoughts	Actions	Physical Responses	Emotions
①				
②				
③				
④				
⑤				
⑥				

My thought log

....

→ Mindfulness and cognitive behavioural techniques

Being in the present and mindfulness are very fashionable terms in current easy living magazines. Every spa and yoga class entices us to take time for ourselves, relax and get in touch with the inner spirit and celebrate being human. Cognitive behavioural therapy and mindfulness have been tremendously successful in helping individuals manage the self-imposed demands of life. This is great news for those of us wishing to balance our activities and find a sense of inner grounding in what could be perceived as a mad, mad world.

We are in a period of transition in the acceptance of and the practising of these philosophies. It can be challenging and take courage to stand up to the external demands on our time. At work, organizations still want us to be as productive but encouragingly some are taking on initiatives which support work/life balance and longevity. We are a long way off though from the universal employment of these values, so it is even more important for us to practise mindfulness for ourselves and for the sake of others.

This is not to say that we should get so lost in the moments and the colour of the leaves that we lose our sense of reality and connection to the world, but with small infusions of 'Time Out', maybe just a few minutes each day, we can increase our sense of well-being.

Noticing things around us reduces anxiety and distracts us from worry and concerns. We all need downtime and if anyone has ever taken a three-week break from normal life you will understand what I mean by allowing yourself to just be and immerse yourself in what's happening now. We can borrow some of this learning and transfer it into everyday living. Finding your balance is key. Your balance will be unique and different to anyone else's.

It is possible to attend mindfulness courses and this is undoubtedly a great way to change everyday habits. For a period of a few hours over eight weeks they will teach you how to suspend self-judgement, accept and be in the present and provide some meditation techniques which are designed for everyday living.

→ Looking after yourself

This chapter may prompt you to **take action** to look after yourself. The tools I have introduced you to so far in this workbook are more centred on everyday practical ways of self-managing as follows:

▶ Tuning into the moment;

▶ Awareness of thoughts related to actions, feelings and physical sensations;

▶ Aiming for compassionate and courageous choices to support you and others;

▶ An increased sense of well-being!

→ Managing our thoughts

Exercise 85:

My mindfulness checklist

Mindfulness involves a conscious direction of our awareness. Have a look at this mindfulness checklist to test yourself on your daily habits. Tick those that you are good at and identify those that you could do more of.

Add your own too!

Daily self-reflective time	Being in the present
Time	Engaging with others
Planning	Engaging with self
Mind-set	Enjoying your surroundings
Energy	Accepting your thoughts and feelings
Focus	Breathing!
Relaxing	
Meditation	
Congratulating yourself	
Adding value	**Time management**
Meaning and purpose	Work/life balance
Selective attention	Time to travel
Making choices	Realistic planning
	Prioritizing

THOUGHTS AND THEIR IMPACT

Some of these daily habits involve awareness of what is happening to us in the moment; if you like, 'paying attention' to our responses.

If we take an example of dieting, most can relate to the negative cycle we can get into of trying, failing and then giving up. Comfort eating is a kind of 'mindless' eating. We can turn to the fridge when feeling negative emotions or stress, but if we break the cycle we can change!

TAPES is a cognitive behavioural tool which you can combine with mindfulness to pay attention to what is happening in the moment, as illustrated in the example below.

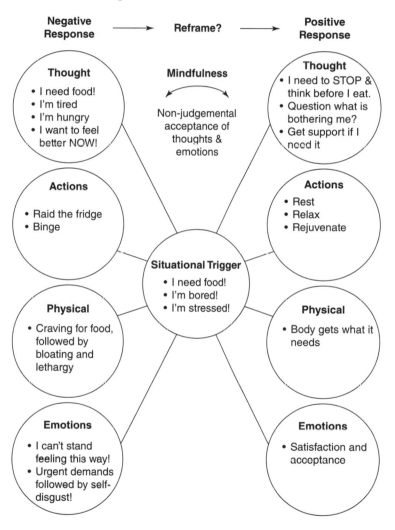

Mindfulness is sometimes described as a non-judgemental state. We don't judge ourselves as good or bad; we just learn to relax into the moment and 'let go' of whatever we might be experiencing.

You will notice that the 'letting go' occurs in between reframing your negative responses to positive. As explored in Chapter 6, it is a state of accepting that there may be some 'guests' in your house. In the case of the food craving example, 'guests' may be 'boredom' or 'stress'. We may allow them to take a seat or leave of their own accord, but we don't have to respond to them, just recognize that they are there. In this accepting or letting go stage, we then create a mindful and peaceful space to move into where we prefer our focus to be. We can then move into the positive reframing stage which may be 'do something' or 'do nothing!'

This workbook aims to stimulate your thoughts and provide you with strategies which will help you focus your energy in a more mindful way.

The idea of the TAPES combined with mindfulness is to increase your ability to practise:

▶ Acceptance

▶ Positive reframing

▶ Self-regulation

Resulting in increased satisfaction in the experience of life!

→ Managing our actions

 **Exercise 86:**

Time and energy

How much time and energy do you put into the following:

Passions?	Engaging with others?
• Interests • Hobbies • Pleasures •	• Relationships • Building networks • Engaging with community • Giving to others • Acts of kindness •
Achieving your goals?	**Meaning and purpose?**
• Short term • Medium term • Long term • Dreams • Ambitions •	• Vocation • Strengths and virtues • Making things happen outside of you •

Describe the things you do:

Passions?	Engaging with others?
•	•
Achieving your goals?	**Meaning and purpose?**
•	•

… and describe the things you would like to do more of:

Passions?	Engaging with others?
•	•
Achieving your goals?	**Meaning and purpose?**
•	•

Turning desires into action

▶ If you would like to do more of something, what has stopped you so far?

_____

_____

_____

_____

▶ What is likely to support you in doing more of this?

_____

_____

_____

_____

▶ What conditions can you create to support you (e.g. people)?

_____

_____

_____

_____

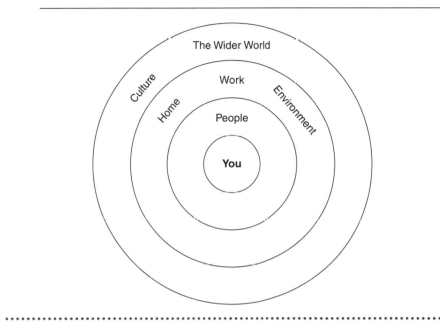

→ Our physical health

Exercise 87:

Managing our physical health

What goals do you have related to your physical well-being? Write them in the grid opposite.

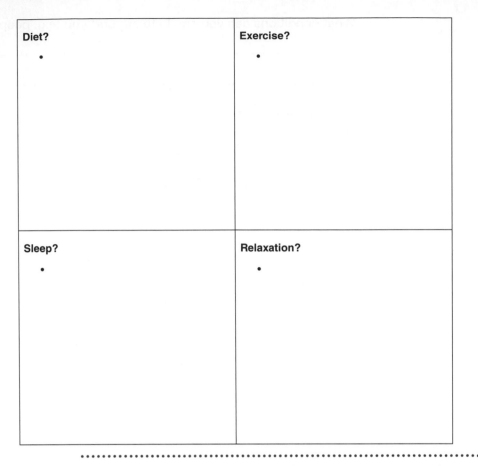

Diet? •	Exercise? •
Sleep? •	Relaxation? •

There is so much research and information about options for improving physical health. If you are concerned about any of these areas there are supports and sources of help available to you some of which are listed here:

Diet

- ▶ General Practitioners
- ▶ Nutritionists
- ▶ Hypnotherapists
- ▶ Herbalists
- ▶ Naturopaths
- ▶ Counsellors
- ▶ Other specialist help, drug, alcohol and other addictions

Exercise/Physical health

- ▶ General practitioner
- ▶ Gym
- ▶ Personal trainer

- ▶ Exercise buddies
- ▶ Osteopaths
- ▶ Chiropractors
- ▶ Reflexology
- ▶ Acupuncture

Sleep
- ▶ General Practitioner
- ▶ Sleep specialists
- ▶ Herbalists
- ▶ Other complementary or alternative therapies

Relaxation
- ▶ Yoga
- ▶ Meditation
- ▶ Hobbies/interests
- ▶ Time with friends/social time

CHOOSING WELL-BEING

What does interest me (and I hope you) is how we make choices about what may be good for us and what gets in the way of those choices.

For some reason in our busy lives when we are under pressure, these things seem to take a low priority at a time when we need to be at our fittest! This suggests that we need to address our priorities in order to build and maintain resilience.

THE BENEFITS OF PHYSICAL WELL-BEING

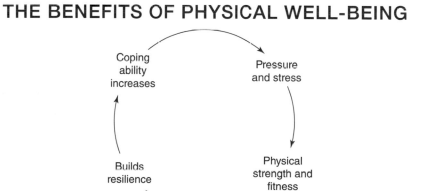

POSSIBLE BLOCKS

▶ Feeling you are worth it

▶ Comfort traps (watching TV versus effort to move)

▶ Habits (autopilot – 'this is what I do')

▶ Negative thinking patterns (e.g. 'I'll do it tomorrow')

▶ Environment and opportunities

I notice that when I'm involved with programmes which offer clients 'well-being' packages, they generally jump at the chance to take up the exercise and look after themselves as if it were the first time they had ever experienced this kind of offering. What an interesting dynamic! I'm guessing that the change in environment creates a mind shift and a conscious space prioritizing physical health.

In order to carry through when developing the well-being mind-set, what we need to do is:

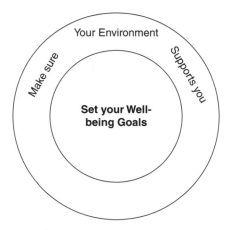

In other words, carry around your own well-being bubble to support you!

Success breeds success, so small steps, one at a time over an extended period will get you there.

If we use the analogy of losing weight, anyone who tracks their successful weight loss over time will probably see a pattern as follows:

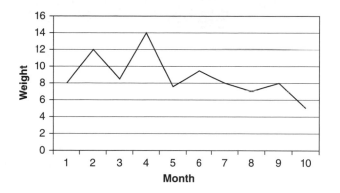

Typically we have lapses and circumstances which prevent us from staying perfectly on track, but it is the overall persistence and not giving up when setbacks occur which get us where we want to be.

The broken cycle can look like this:

Try/fail cycle

What we want to create is this realistic 'Cycle of success!'

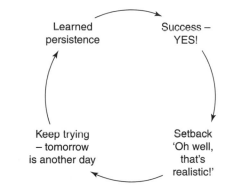

Cycle of success

→ Sleep

I want to mention sleep here as so many people worry about sleep. The anxiety about not getting sleep then creates more sleeplessness!

 **Exercise 88:**

My sleep

Here are a few questions to ask yourself about your sleep:

▶ How many hours do I get regularly?

_____

_____

▶ How many do I need?

_____

_____

▶ What interrupts my sleep?

_____

_____

▶ What are my energy levels like during the day?

_____

_____

▶ How regular are my sleep patterns?

_____

_____

A few things to consider:

▶ **It is normal to have a few interruptions to sleep during the night.**

▶ **We can cope with missing the odd night's sleep.**

▶ **Unresolved issues can interrupt sleep – make a plan to address the issues at the appropriate time rather than in the middle of the night!**

Apply mindfulness to calm your mind and so aid getting to sleep.

A SLEEP EXERCISE

As you are settling to sleep, get into a comfortable physical position and relax your jaws.

Now, concentrating on your breathing, start to breathe in and out slowly to the count of 3, then 10.

If you have thoughts entering in, acknowledge them, let them drift, then come back to your counting and breathing.

The longer the breaths, the more relaxed you will feel …

DISTRACTION

If you can't sleep, know that you have other options:

▶ A warm drink

▶ A book

▶ Music

▶ Relaxation tape or something that distracts you and relaxes you.

→ Your emotions

My emotions

▶ How are you feeling right now?

Positive emotions?	Mood?
Negative emotions?	Overall satisfaction feeling?

▶ Why are you feeling this particular way?

Positive emotions?	Mood?
Negative emotions?	Overall satisfaction feeling?

....

You may get clues to this from the **Wheel of Well-Being** connections shown earlier in this chapter, or some small happening(s) today may have influenced your mood.

Feelings provide important feedback if we pay attention to them. Sometimes they can spiral up or down. If left unchecked they can be subject to:

- ▶ Over generalization (Everything is terrible!)
- ▶ Distortion (I am late, so will lose my job!)
- ▶ Deletion (My achievement was nothing really)
- ▶ … and other barriers to positive thinking, including the **'Inner critics visiting through the back door!'**

Managing emotions and self-regulating is a skill we can learn. The TAPES help us to make connections to the whole self.

→ Emotions and their power

Sometimes our emotions, physical tiredness or the **'last straw'** can get in the way and we can feel emotional on one day and then completely calm the following day.

LEARNING TO REGULATE EMOTIONS

- ▶ If too upset or angry to respond to a situation, distract yourself by moving away to give yourself time to calm down and think more clearly.
- ▶ Get the facts. Make sure you understand the situation. Don't jump to conclusions.
- ▶ Talk it out with sympathetic and objective others.
- ▶ Don't let negative thoughts run away with you.
- ▶ Detach. Step back and watch yourself. Go into observer mode.
- ▶ Sit with the thoughts or feelings; use mindfulness to observe them. Perhaps it isn't what you thought first. Some emotions are more than one layer; something different might be seen underneath if you observe carefully. Remind yourself of your core values. Don't do something that's going to hurt people that you love.
- ▶ Resist emotional behaviour. Impulsive, emotional behaviour maintains or heightens the unwanted emotion and usually leads to adverse consequences. Doing nothing is usually better than doing something stupid.
- ▶ Counter physiological arousal. If too excited, scared or angry, use relaxation exercises to calm you down. If too lethargic, bored or detached, do something like exercise or move around.
- ▶ Refocus attention. Distract yourself from upsetting emotions through physical or mental activity – 'move a muscle, change a thought.'
- ▶ Do something useful. Accomplish something else, something that is of value to you and is not related to the upsetting emotion.

When we are feeling emotional it is difficult to 'think' straight, especially if we are in the fight/flight/freeze mode. Calming down and using breathing helps us self-regulate, relax and re-group. Perspective and awareness are great relievers of stress. I have prepared some relaxation exercises which you can practise anywhere and are quick, but effective.

They are:

▶ SAFE – a brief imaginary journey to distract and calm

▶ PEACE – a meditative calming exercise

▶ Breathing exercise – for physical relaxation

SAFE – A RELAXATION EXERCISE – ESCAPE ON AN IMAGINARY JOURNEY

Find a comfortable place where you can sit or lie down comfortably without interruptions.

If necessary let others know you are not available.

Close your eyes and breathe slowly in and out for a few minutes.

Imagine you are in a very special, safe place which to you represents rest, peace and relaxation …

S	See	Notice what you can see. Create that picture in your mind of your very special place. Look around you very slowly and notice the details one by one…
A	Audio	Hear the sounds, turn the volume up and then down for each sound in turn and then allow them to all merge together….
F	Feel	Feel yourself relax even more as you enjoy your surroundings and soak in the warm, safe feelings knowing that you are in your own special place…
E	Experience	Enjoy the experience of just being accepting of your very special 'safe place'…

When you are ready, allow yourself to become aware where you are sitting or lying and your surroundings.

Slowly leave your 'safe place' taking all your good feelings with you, open your eyes and re-enter the world around you.

PEACE – A MEDITATIVE CALMING EXERCISE

P	Physical	I'm breathing in and out slowly, my body is relaxed. I am at PEACE
E	Emotional	I'm feeling calm. I am at PEACE
A	Action	I'm doing things at my own pace. I am at PEACE
C	Cognitive	I'm thinking realistically and positively. I am at PEACE
E	Event	Whatever happens around me, I can choose how I respond. I am at PEACE

BREATHING EXERCISE

▶ Find a place to sit quietly if you can

▶ Look around you and notice what you can see, hear, and feel

▶ Start to notice how you are breathing

▶ Allow your surroundings to come and go, and then bring your attention back to your breathing

▶ As you slow your breathing, breathe in for 3 seconds, then out for 3 seconds.

▶ Repeat this again a few times until you feel you are breathing rhythmically.

▶ As your body relaxes, breathe in again this time for 5 seconds and again out for 5 seconds. In and out, again and again.

▶ Allow yourself to pause between breaths for a few seconds.

▶ Feel your heart slow down and experience a release of tension in your body as you continue to breathe in and out slowly and easily.

▶ As you breathe, notice the sounds, what you can see and how you can feel at one and present with your surroundings, yet relaxed and able to continue taking this good feeling with you.

→ **Doing the things you love**

The things I love to do!

As this chapter is about well-being, let's end by reminding you of all the things you love to do!

List them, don't worry about how random they are just let them flow ...

_____

_____

_____

_____

_____

_____

_____

_____

_____

_____

And step into your well-being bubble!

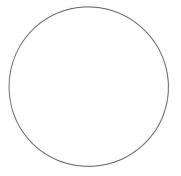

Summary

- ▶ The wheel of well-being captures recommendations to support happiness and increase well-being.
- ▶ Our feelings are an important source of feedback.
- ▶ Mindfulness and cognitive behavioural therapy can help with depression and well-being.
- ▶ Making change happen involves trying, failing and learning from setbacks.
- ▶ Sleep = stress release.
- ▶ Doing more of what we love takes mindful application!

My learnings from this chapter

_____

_____

_____

_____

_____

_____

Positive thoughts

_____

_____

_____

_____

_____

_____

Where to next

In the next chapter we will be putting it all together and you will be thinking about the actions that you would like to put in place.

Putting it all together

We have navigated our way through this workbook together and I hope you already have some useful tools and ideas for managing stress and developing resilience.

Herein lies the biggest challenge you have in making personal change happen. On the one hand we may be operating under difficult circumstances, but on the other hand is it inevitable how we react to those events or circumstances?

This is where we look at the vision for the future and translate future desires into sustained actions with supports, anchors and rewards.

→ Managing stress and developing resilience

Here's a reminder of the areas we have covered so far:

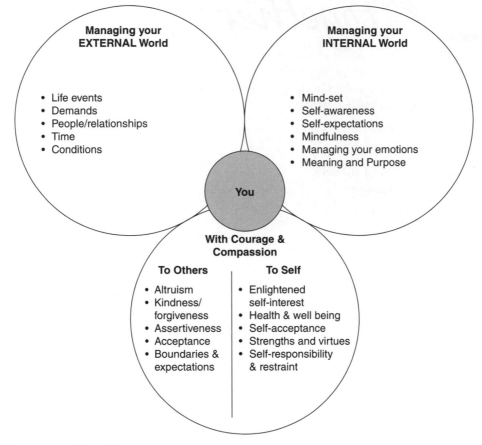

Managing your EXTERNAL World
- Life events
- Demands
- People/relationships
- Time
- Conditions

Managing your INTERNAL World
- Mind-set
- Self-awareness
- Self-expectations
- Mindfulness
- Managing your emotions
- Meaning and Purpose

You

With Courage & Compassion

To Others
- Altruism
- Kindness/ forgiveness
- Assertiveness
- Acceptance
- Boundaries & expectations

To Self
- Enlightened self-interest
- Health & well being
- Self-acceptance
- Strengths and virtues
- Self-responsibility & restraint

The self-management model

In other words self-managing your external and internal worlds with courage and compassion will help you feel more resilient and fulfilled. It will also help you feel more energized to give willingly to others.

→ Managing stress positively

Managing stress positively involves being mindful about the following:

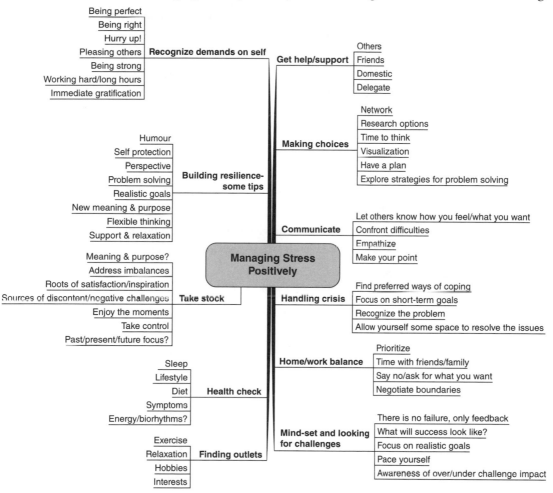

→ Some of my key messages with visual anchors (reminders)

ANCHORS

Anchors are reminders which can be visual, physical, emotional or cognitive. By association, your chosen anchors can quickly remind you in the moment about important messages you wish to recall. Anchors can help you change behaviours mindfully. Examples of anchors are:

▶ Physical – e.g. a squeeze of the forefinger and the thumb or slow breathing or squeezing an object in your pocket;

- Visual – e.g. a mental image or screensaver or picture on your wall;
- Emotional – e.g. affirmations of positive memories and association with positive emotions;
- Sensing – e.g. using memories and the imagination related to smell, taste, touch, sounds;
- Cognitive – e.g. positive thoughts and affirmations such as 'I will do my best and deal with the unexpected as it arises'
- Practical reminders – e.g. a message on your phone, your wall, your computer, in your drawer. A letter or message to yourself to pop up as a reminder.

These are a few examples, but what matters is that your anchors have meaning to you.

Visual anchors

Let's practise with some visual anchors in relation to some key messages. Create your own images in the blanks below:

Visual anchor	Key message
	• Know and act on what's good for you – identify the gaps and make wise choices!
	• Be aware of impulse and immediate gratification habits – first, if you know you're in this space admit it! Second get support!
	• Loss – you will never know when you're over it, but by looking after yourself and investing in yourself, each day will get a little brighter over time and newness will emerge.
	• In crisis and with accumulated stress, it is sometimes the last straw which tips the balance. Resist the emotional urge to charge at it and go in like a bull in a china shop (fight response) or bury your head in the sand and hope the storm passes. Take stock and mindfully ask yourself what can you do?
	• Keep perspective – what's the worst that can happen? Count your blessings. Does it pass the 'So what?' test in the grand scale of things?
	• Ask yourself the question, what's in my control/out of my control? Focusing your energy on what's out of your control will exhaust you. Let it go! Focus on the small significant things you can influence.

	· Have a plan and focus.
	· Inform others/involve others, build your relationships.
	· When you're climbing out of the abyss one step at a time, one foot in front of the other, day to day, longer steps and evidence of your progress will emerge later.
	· Take time to reflect – even if there's no time!
	· Avoid running around in circles.
	· Celebrate small wins and congratulate yourself for surviving difficulties.
	· Have a plan 'A', 'B' and 'C' if it helps, but be prepared to be flexible with your thinking and actions when circumstances change.
	· Review what you are doing, learning, changing – use resources/skills you have, but be open to developing new ones too!
	· Adjust your mind-set to adapt to your current situation.
	· In crisis, exercise damage limitation. Protect and keep safe what you can – accept what you could lose at worst. You are then dealing with reality.
	· Look for opportunities for newness emerging, be open to it when it comes to you – be willing to try/experiment – you know you have a fall-back position and can learn from experience.
	· Enjoy meaningful pleasures every day.
	· Get support – accept support – don't be proud, be grateful!
	· Accept that life has ups and downs (and nobody escapes them).
	· Don't compare yourself with others. Who they are and what they do is their business. You can enjoy the positive impact they have on your life. Accept their flaws and support them when they are down, but you don't have to be them or follow their rules of life. Wear the 'Me' t-shirt.
	· Be realistic, pace yourself, manage your self-demands and develop a positive healthy mind-set.
	· Be confident in the knowledge that you do have the resources or can develop them!

→ Here's a process for responding to challenge and looking for opportunities

An example of a challenge/opportunity may be preparing for a presentation or an interview and dealing with performance nerves and anxiety:

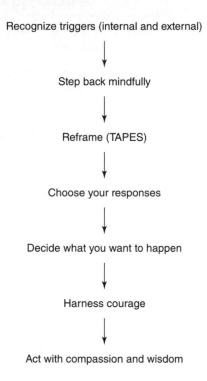

Recognize triggers (internal and external)

↓

Step back mindfully

↓

Reframe (TAPES)

↓

Choose your responses

↓

Decide what you want to happen

↓

Harness courage

↓

Act with compassion and wisdom

Translated into TAPES this looks like:

→ Planning to perform – TAPES example

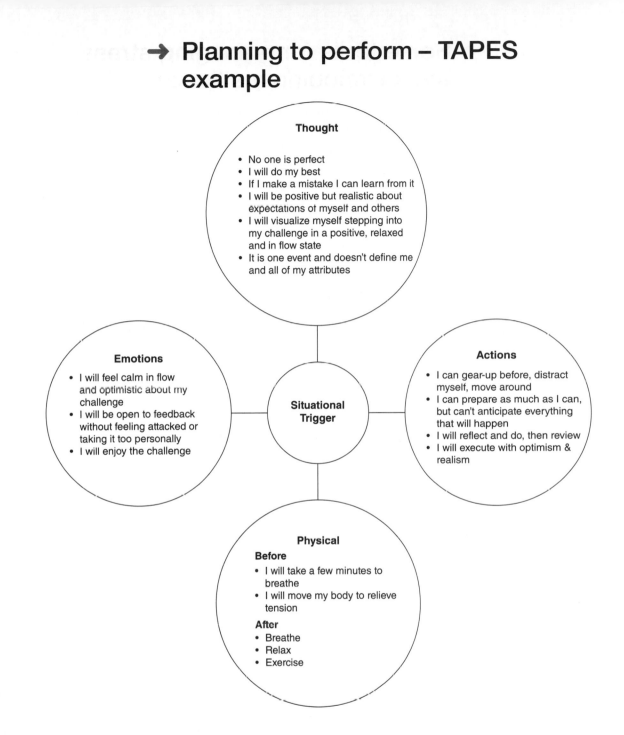

Thought

- No one is perfect
- I will do my best
- If I make a mistake I can learn from it
- I will be positive but realistic about expectations of myself and others
- I will visualize myself stepping into my challenge in a positive, relaxed and in flow state
- It is one event and doesn't define me and all of my attributes

Emotions

- I will feel calm in flow and optimistic about my challenge
- I will be open to feedback without feeling attacked or taking it too personally
- I will enjoy the challenge

Situational Trigger

Actions

- I can gear-up before, distract myself, move around
- I can prepare as much as I can, but can't anticipate everything that will happen
- I will reflect and do, then review
- I will execute with optimism & realism

Physical

Before
- I will take a few minutes to breathe
- I will move my body to relieve tension

After
- Breathe
- Relax
- Exercise

➔ Some tools for managing stress and developing resilience

Here are a few of the tools you have explored in this workbook already to help you along the way:

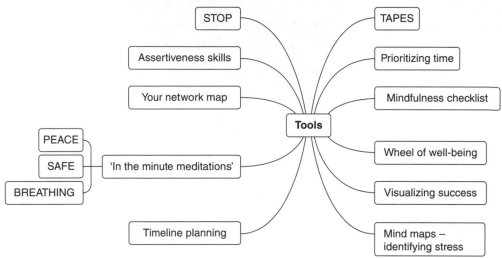

➔ The resilience bubble

The more strategies we have to support us in managing stress, the stronger and more confident we become. The five stages in developing resilience are:

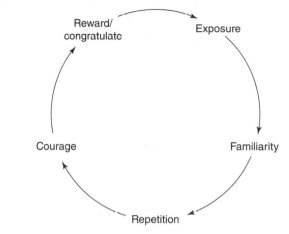

Reward/congratulate → Exposure → Familiarity → Repetition → Courage

Resilience checklist

With every experience we believe we have handled well we expand our confidence and resilience bubbles and develop resources we can draw on.

Each time we feel success we must congratulate and celebrate to embed our own confidence, even when the conditions are at their worst!

Complete this self-check to reflect on how well you are managing the development of your own resilience:

		Could do more of?	Yes/No?
Exposure (Stretch)	• New challenges • Am I taking enough measured risks? • I taking on too many risks?		

Exposure (Resolution)	· Unresolved issues – am I dealing with unresolved issues?		
Exposure (Goals)	· Am I setting myself realistic goals? · Are they relevant to my short and long term?		
Familiarity	· Am I exposing myself to opportunities for becoming familiar with challenges? · Am I trying enough? · Am I trying too hard?		
Repetition	· Do I have enough supports and reminders to help me? · Am I practising everyday habits to develop my skills? · Do I take time out to review my focus, learning and direction?		
Courage	· Am I harnessing my courage to gear up for challenges? · Do I have the tools to help me use my courage? · Do I have the support I need?		
Rewards	· Am I noting what I achieve/do well? · Am I actively celebrating and enjoying success? · Am I capturing my learning?		

→ Vision – your desires

Your personal vision

You have analysed a great deal of information in this workbook. Now let's explore and tap into your creative right brain. The right side of the brain is where much of our creativity comes from; the left side is the more analytical side. You don't have to be Picasso or Rembrandt to do this exercise; we all have some creativity which is sometimes blocked by language. If it helps, close your eyes and breathe in and out slowly for a few minutes until inspiration comes to you and then just go with the flow.

Now

Draw a picture of how you see yourself in your whole situation/life now (using no words):

The future

Now draw a picture of how you would like to see yourself in your situation/life at some point in the future (using no words) – the future may be when you choose but I suggest within two years as it is harder to see beyond then:

What do you see in your pictures and how does it inform you about your life and your desires?

Notes

_____

_____

_____

_____

_____

_____

_____

_____

_____

. . . .

MAKING IT HAPPEN – A RECIPE FOR ACTION:

What really matters at this point is that we turn desires into solid practical actions!

Here are my recommendations for turning desires into reality. There are ten steps involved.

→ 10-step change guide

1 Identify your goals;

2 Visualize success and what success will look like;

3 Timeline your journey – work from the end-point backwards – timeline planning;

4 Define actions – describe in the positive: 'I will … ';

5 Plan for a positive mind-set – capture with TAPES, recognize practical or psychological blocks;

6 Craft your environment to support you as far as you can;

7 Supports – reach out to others to help you – you can help them too;

8 Congratulate and reward yourself on your achievements;

9 Review what went well – capture the things you were proud of and log them;

10 Place your new learnings and resources into your toolkit. You can use this kit at any time!

ONE STEP AT A TIME!

We can only do so much at once so I recommend you take one step at a time. If you repeat the behaviour you're aiming for as often as you can, the more a behaviour is repeated, the more likely it is that it will become 'instinctive'. Daily mindful practice will get you there.

So choosing your goals carefully is important. Sometimes small changes lead to high impact, so being creative about how you form your goals will be key to ensure you are successful in making change happen.

We will go through each of these steps in turn to transform your goals into real actions!

STEP 1 IDENTIFY YOUR GOALS

You have captured many thoughts and learnings throughout this book so now might be a good time to scan through them to remind yourself of their significance.

You have also explored your personal vision of the future which you can use as inspiration for your goals. You now have an opportunity to choose what is most important to you and to break those desires down into practical things you can do to make them happen.

So what are your goals? I would suggest you focus on two to three at a time so that you don't become overwhelmed, but you may want to summarize your goals on the model I asked you to start thinking about in Chapter 2 :

Exercise 93:

Summary of my goals

Use this grid to capture where you wish to focus your energy in the future (an inventory of your goals). List those things important to you specifically:

Home	Passions
Work	**Meaning and Purpose**

Now from your summary of goals pick two to three you wish to start working on. Make your goals SMART – a widely accepted business acronym for making your goals:

- ▶ **Specific**
- ▶ **Measurable**
- ▶ **Achievable**
- ▶ **Realistic**
- ▶ **Time-based**

Describe them here (smartly!)

▶ _____

_____

_____

_____

▶ _____

_____

_____

_____

▶ _____

_____

_____

_____

STEP 2 VISUALIZE SUCCESS: WHAT WILL SUCCESS LOOK LIKE?

We are going to warm up to this idea of visualizing success with the following exercise where you engage **your past and future self**.

Think about something you made happen successfully in the past.

Then think about one of your future goals.

Work through this exercise:

 *Exercise 94:*

Engaging your past and future self – visualizing success

What is your goal?

Describe one of your goals relating to a future challenge:

_____

_____

_____

_____

_____

_____

Anchor (sensing)

Choose an object or a form of touch which you will use immediately after you recollect your positive goals below:

_____

Past success

Pick a time when you have had a **positive/successful** experience with either a similar or different goal:

Close your eyes and recollect:

▶ **What were you thinking?**

_____

_____

_____

▶ What were you doing?

_____

_____

_____

▶ What were you sensing (seeing, hearing, touch, smell, taste)?

_____

_____

_____

▶ How was your input or the result of your efforts received?

_____

_____

_____

▶ How did you feel?

_____

_____

_____

Anchor

Now anchor that good feeling with your chosen object or touch. Breathe, relax and enjoy that feeling for 30 seconds.

When you are ready, open your eyes.

Future

Now using your past positive experience as a resource, fast forward to your future successful self-facing your challenge. Close your eyes and imagine:

▶ What are you thinking?

_____

_____

_____

▶ What are you doing?

_____

_____

_____

▶ What are you sensing?

_____

_____

_____

▶ How is your input or the results of your efforts received?

_____

_____

_____

▶ How do you feel?

_____

_____

Anchor

Anchor that good feeling and enjoy for 30 seconds.

Open your eyes and release your anchor! Every time you wish to remind yourself of these positive feelings you can use your anchor.

 The powers of the imagination, together with the power of evidence of past successes are a formidable energy source!

You can use this exercise to:

▶ gear-up for a challenge

▶ make plans for how you wish to approach a challenge

▶ think about how you reframe your thoughts positively as part of reframing.

STEP 3 TIMELINE YOUR JOURNEY

Timeline of your journey

Now taking the example you have just worked through create a timeline identifying what success will look like at the end of the timeframe and work back along your timeline, plotting the actions which will need to happen at the different points to make this goal happen:

STEP 4 DEFINE ACTIONS

From your timeline you can now see clearly the specific actions required.

My action plan

List those actions, describing what you **will** do and the measures for success as follows (you can complete the column on 'supports' once you have read Step 7):

My personal action plan

My goal:

My vision:

_____

Actions (What I will do)	How I will do it? (Steps to take)	Supports? (People and environment)	Review Has it worked? – Yes/no /in part?	Timeframe (How long to change?)
Action step 1				
Action step 2				
Action step 3				
Action step 4				
Action step 5				
Action step 6				

You can complete this process for each of your goals.

STEP 5 PLAN FOR A POSITIVE MIND-SET

We have explored how we can sometimes get in the way of ourselves by negative thinking and how we can reframe towards positive thinking.

Handling a relationship conflict, for example, may need some careful planning and self-restraint before taking action. Planning for the knee-jerk responses and our hot buttons are our potential internal friends and supporters!

It may help to capture a summary of your potential negative and your positive reframed thoughts which you have accumulated throughout this workbook (some may already be identified in your 'positive thoughts' space at the end of each chapter. This will create a quick reference guide in those hot button moments and you can acknowledge your inner critics and supporters – 'Oh its him/her/it again!'

Capture your summary of negative and positive thoughts here:

_____

_____

_____

_____

_____

_____

_____

_____

_____

_____

_____

_____

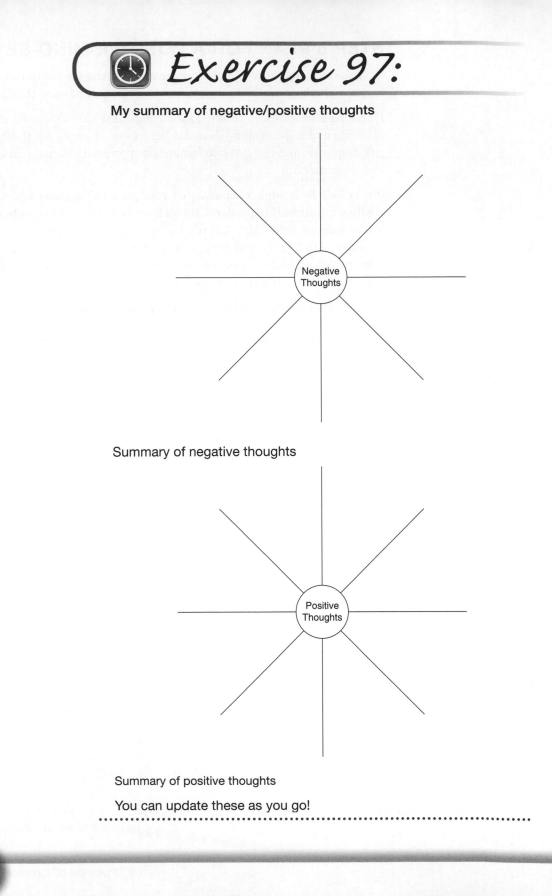

Exercise 97:

My summary of negative/positive thoughts

Negative
Thoughts

Summary of negative thoughts

Positive
Thoughts

Summary of positive thoughts

You can update these as you go!

STEP 6 CRAFT YOUR ENVIRONMENT

In **Chapter 1** you considered your external environment. Let's revisit that and think about whether you would like to adapt or alter anything related to your external environment to support you in making change happen. If you want to do more exercise you may sign up at the gym; if you want to make more time for yourself you may need to adjust the time you spend in different environments; if you want to expand your social network you may wish to consider how and where.

EXAMPLES OF ENVIRONMENTS:

- ▶ Countryside
- ▶ Nature
- ▶ Towns/cities
- ▶ Home
- ▶ Gardens
- ▶ Hobbies
- ▶ Interests
- ▶ Sanctuary
- ▶ Busy
- ▶ Community
- ▶ Library
- ▶ Universities/colleges
- ▶ Gym

Draw into the diagram below the influences which you may wish to change in your external world.

Crafting my environment

For example:

- Where you live?

- Within your culture?

- Your community and social life?

- Work environment?

- Other things which influence your external world?

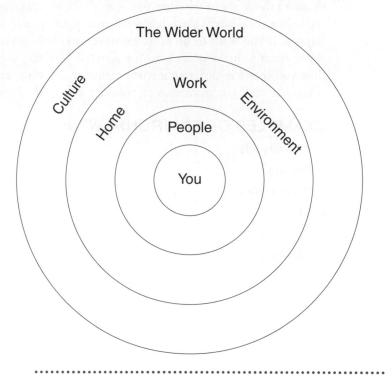

The Wider World

Culture

Work

Home

Environment

People

You

STEP 7 SUPPORTS AND REACHING OUT ...

We tend to think of supports as people we share our goals with. Support for you making changes may come in many different forms:

▶ People
▶ Mentors
▶ Loved ones
▶ Family
▶ Friends
▶ Co-workers
▶ Clubs
▶ Animals
▶ Neighbours
▶ Community

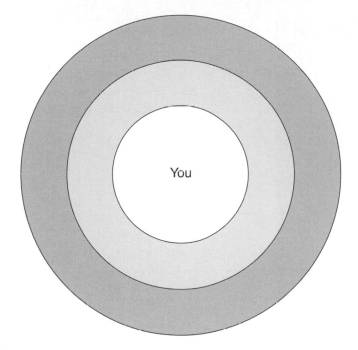

We have different relationships for different reasons. Developing trusted supporters can really help and you may be able to support them too. Include loved ones in your plans and get their buy-in; the 'what's in it for them' will build your chances of success and help them achieve their desires and ambitions too. Remember win/win!

Identify those you could reach out to both in your environment and for support here:

What I will do? (Action point)	How I will do it? (Steps to take)	Supports? (Environment and people))	Review Has it worked? – (Yes/no/in part?	Time frame (How long to change?)
Action step 1				
Action step 2				

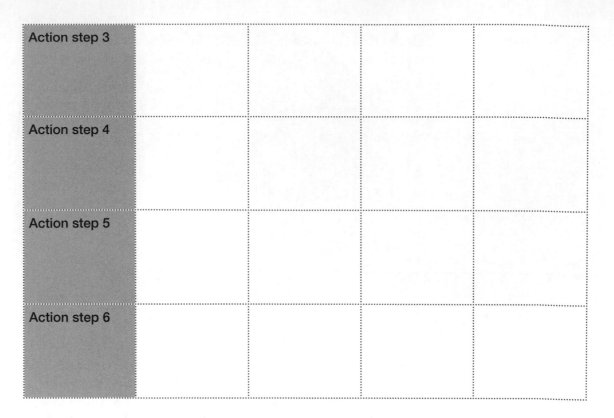

Action step 3				
Action step 4				
Action step 5				
Action step 6				

STEP 8 CONGRATULATE YOURSELF!

Now that you have your plan all you need to do is do it!

Then when you are successful congratulate yourself and celebrate it!

Celebration involves:

▶ Acknowledging your achievements

▶ Recognizing the effort you put in to making it happen

▶ Enjoying the moments both in the journey and basking in your success

▶ Rewarding yourself with some time and energy focused on you doing the things you love to do

▶ Sharing and celebrating with others

STEP 9 REVIEWING

This is the learning from experience stage. Taking time out to think about or discuss with others what your journey has been like. Life is a series of journeys so joining the dots brings great insight and helps us think about how we navigate through. With wisdom we can transcend beyond just existing or responding to events towards embracing and living life to the full.

STEP 10 CREATING YOUR RESOURCE TOOLBOX

The more you create opportunities for learning the greater your potential to add to your personal power and your toolbox of resources.

YOUR VIRTUOUS CIRCLE

With tools and vision you can create your own virtuous circle.

Your virtuous circle relies on you investing in yourself and then success breeds success. If we try and then give up because we are put off by the inevitable setbacks which occur when we are trying something new, we create a negative spiral and a learned helplessness.

By turning your back on this idea and moving into a positive space, which is about trying and learning and being kind to yourself in the process, you create a positive spiral. The virtuous circle is the bigger picture of many positive spirals coming together and creating amazing confidence. We may not know everything but we can feel confident about trying!

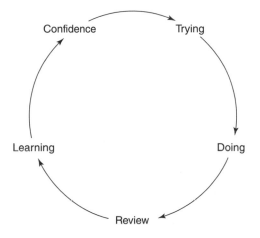

Summary

▶ Managing stress and developing resilience involves managing our external and internal worlds with courage and compassion.

▶ Anchors are useful reminders for making changes.

▶ The TAPES model will help you reframe your thoughts, actions, physical responses and emotions from negative to positive.

▶ You can develop your resilience through exposure, familiarity and repetition, not forgetting courage, compassion and rewards!

▶ The 10-step guide to change will help you make change happen!

My learnings from this chapter

_____

_____

_____

_____

_____

_____

Positive thoughts

_____

_____

_____

_____

_____

_____

Some final messages

Are you feeling hopeful about the future? I hope that whatever circumstances you find yourself in you can transcend them, look at the big picture and make wise choices for yourself and for the benefit of others.

We are living in perpetually changing times and life can throw curve balls at us sometimes. This is all the more reason to be kind to ourselves, be our own best friend and create a ripple of well-being around us. Our future success depends on us using our wisdom rather than impulse and our present is there for the taking. We can make choices too about what we let go of from the past and what we take with us going forward. We live in an amazing world of opportunities and experiences if we stop to notice them.

Embracing life is the essence of this book.

It's goodbye from me!

Writing this workbook has been an incredible adventure for me and, of course, we have to manage endings to create new beginnings.

I am leaving you the gift of my toolbox, which I hope will now become yours.

We have come to the end of our experience together and I hope you have found it a useful and engaging one. I am always inspired by the ability of others to turn adversity into an opportunity: the power to do this exists in all of us.

I wish you happiness, fulfilment and hope in whatever choices you make!

References

Bowlby, J. *A Secure Base: Parent-Child Attachment and Healthy Human Development* (Routledge, 1988)

Campbell, Dr S. *Saying What's Real: Seven Keys to Authentic Communication and Relationship Success* (New World Library, 2003)

Costa, P. T. Jr. and McCrae, R. R. *NEO Personality Inventory* (Psychological Assessment Resources, Inc., 2010)

Darwin, C. R. *On the Origin of Species* (John Murray, 1859)

Friedman, M. *Type A Behaviour: Its Diagnosis and Treatment* (1996)

Hykel-Hunt, Mary *Learning from the Future* (self-published 2011)

Kolb, D. A. and Fry, R. *Toward an applied theory of experiential learning* (John Wiley, 1975)

Lazarus, R. S. *Personality and Adjustment* (Prentice-Hall, 1963)

Maslow, A. H. *A Theory of Human Motivation* (self-published, 1943)

McIntosh, B. J. *Spoiled Child Syndrome* (Official Journal of Paediatrics, 1989)

Mehrabian, A. *Silent Messages: Implicit Communication of Emotions and Attitudes* (2nd ed. Wadsworth, 1981)

Seligman, M. E. P. *Authentic Happiness: Using the New Positive Psychology to Realize Your Potential for Lasting Fulfilment* (Simon and Schuster, 2002)

Selye, H. *Stress without distress* (J. B. Lippincott Co., 1974)

Index